would you survive being sucked into a black hole? ✝ Einstein's brain lives on in 240 slices ✝ **unbelievable** man who survived chopper blades ✝ bacteria that makes electricity ✝ the 10,000-mile-long toilet could poison gas save our lives? ✝ would you survive being sucked has a black hole? ✝ the man who saved himself ✝ India is sinking ✝ the gambler who broke Monte Carlo ✝ swallowing molten lead and surviving ✝ gross ways to stay alive in the wild ✝ levitating frog **stories** ✝ man's tattoo puts him in jail ✝ joking disease ✝ how to make wine out of seagulls ✝ farmer cures horse with beer ✝ living with a hole in your stomach ✝ ghost yachts ✝ bacteria that creates electricity ✝ could poison gas save peoples lives? ✝ **for guys** ⋏

Ripley's

Believe It or Not!®

lightning killed an entire football team

PUBLISHING

Publisher Anne Marshall

Editorial Director Rebecca Miles
Senior Researcher & Picture Manager James Proud
Text James Proud, Geoff Tibballs
Proofreader Sally McFall
Factchecker Justin Audibert

Art Director Sam South
Design Michelle Foster
Reprographics Juice Creative

Executive VP Norm Deska
VP, Exhibits & Archives Edward Meyer

For information regarding permission, write to VP Intellectual Property Ripley Entertainment Inc. Suite 188, 7576 Kingspointe Parkway Orlando, Florida 32819

email: publishing@ripleys.com
www.ripleybooks.com

Published by Ripley Publishing 2012
Ripley Publishing, Suite 188,
7576 Kingspointe Parkway,
Orlando, Florida 32819, USA

2 4 6 8 10 9 7 5 3 1

ISBN: 978-1-60991-013-6

Library of Congress Cataloging-in-Publication Data
Proud, James.
  Ripley's believe it or not! : unbelievable stories for guys / [text, James Proud, Geoff Tibballs].
    p. cm.
  Includes bibliographical references and index.
  ISBN 978-1-60991-013-6
1. Curiosities and wonders. I. Tibballs, Geoff. II. Title.
  AG243.P76 2012
  031.02--dc23

2012000228

Manufactured in China
in January/2012 by Leo Paper
1st printing

First published in Great Britain in 2012 by Random House Books, Random House, 20 Vauxhall Bridge Road, London SW1V 2SA

www.randomhouse.co.uk

Addresses for companies within The Random House Group Limited can be found at www.randomhouse.co.uk/offices/htm

The Random House Group Limited Reg. No. 954009

A CIP catalogue record for this book is available from the British Library

ISBN 9781847946928 (UK)

PUBLISHER'S NOTE
While every effort has been made to verify the accuracy of the entries in this book, the Publishers cannot be held responsible for any errors contained in the work. They would be glad to receive any information from readers.

WARNING
Some of the stunts and activities in this book are undertaken by experts and should not be attempted by anyone without adequate training and supervision.

would you survive being sucked into a black hole? † Einstein's brain lives on in 240 slices **unbelievable** man who survived chopper blades † bacteria that makes electricity † the 10,000-mile-long toilet could poison gas save our lives? † would you survive being sucked into a black hole? † Einstein himself † India is sinking † the gambler who broke Monte Carlo † swallowing molten lead and surviving † gross ways to stay alive in the wild † levitating frog **stories** † man's tattoo puts him in jail † joking disease † how to make wine out of seagulls † farmer cures horse with beer † living with a hole in ghost yachts † bacteria electricity † could poison lives? † **for guys** †

Ripley's

Believe *It or Not!*

Ripley
PUBLISHING
a Jim Pattison Company

lightning killed an entire soccer team

“I have made a living out of the fact that truth is stranger than fiction”

Ripley

“ BELIEVE IT OR NOT ”

Contents

An unbelievable guy

The great Robert Ripley said that he'd been called a liar more often than probably anybody else on Earth and that he would never have it any other way! More than brushing off the insult, he thrived on it, turning it into a compliment. Being called a liar, he judged, meant that he'd found a fact, stumbled on a story, taken a photograph of something that was scarcely believable. The possibility of finding a gem of a story that was wildly strange but true was the very motivation for his tireless journeys around the globe.

In 1918, Ripley began recording his findings in his daily cartoon on *The New York Globe*. The Ripley's Believe It or Not! cartoon was a runaway success—every day 3,500 letters were delivered to Ripley's desk from adoring fans responding to the cartoon's provocative subject matter. Who wouldn't react to such tempting topics as "the river of vinegar," "the boy with owl eyes," or to Ripley's assertion that Aesop did not write *Aesop's Fables*?

The extraordinary came naturally to Robert Ripley—he lived his whole life as a BION (Believe It or Not) story. Just one glance at his own record of the miles he traveled—exceptional distances for the period—exposes his dedication to the pursuit of the weird.

Around the U.S. and Mexico	Up to 1920	*80,000 miles*
Trip to Europe	1920	*11,000*
Europe and the Holy Land	1921	*12,000*
Europe	1922	*10,000*
West Indies	1923	*8,000*
Round the world	1924	*37,000*
Round South America	1926	*27,000*
West Indies and Mexico	1926	*11,000*
Europe	1926	*13,000*
Scandinavia	1927	*16,000*
Mexico and Central America	1928	*18,000*
Europe	1928	*11,000*
North Africa and the Holy Land	1929–30	*19,000*
Europe	1931	*12,000*
Newfoundland and Nova Scotia	1931	*4,000*
South Seas and the Orient	1932	*23,000*
Europe	1932	*11,000*
Europe (small countries)	1932	*14,000*
Africa and South America	1933	*36,000*
Persia and Russia	1933	*27,000*
Miscellaneous in US and Canada	1929–33	*64,000*
Total		*464,000 miles*

This total mileage is equal to more than 16 times around the world at the Equator and more than the distance from Earth to the Moon and back.

Note: In addition to these trips recorded by Ripley himself, he continued to travel extensively until 1940.

Today, at Ripley's, as we prepare the *Ripley's Believe It or Not!* books and hunt for new exhibits for the 31 Ripley Odditoriums (museums) around the world, we sift through mountains of bizarre photographs, news stories and submissions to uncover peculiar artifacts and people who live life on the far side. Kids (and big kids) love the books' images of giant burgers, the longest cat, the black-tie dinner party held on Everest, and the like. But among the attention-grabbing photographs are stupendous stories that don't need visuals to make an impact. When featured in our publications, these sometimes "grown-up" stories are often censored and kept tantalizingly short. We think some of these overlooked gems deserve a stage of their own. So here they are!

Unbelievable Stories for Guys are shocking tales for adults celebrating unbelievable, often dark and cringing facts. These are stories deemed too extreme, profane, repugnant or complex for our other publications, or the daily Ripley's Believe It or Not! cartoon, syndicated around the world for 90 years. We've dug deep for a host of original oddities, hard to swallow trivia, bizarre lists that we think guys will find fascinating. We provide answers to questions they never knew they had. Look out for London's railway for the dead and the Russian who survived putting his head in a particle accelerator. Did you know that the first Porsche was a hybrid? Would cockroaches *really* be the last things standing after the apocalypse?

James Proud
Senior Researcher

The first Porsche was a hybrid The first production Porsche sports car, designed by the Austrian Ferdinand Porsche and built in 1900, was a hybrid. The Lohner-Porsche Semper Vivus used a gasoline engine, electric motors and a battery and could reach 35 mph (56 km/h), an Austrian record at that time. It would be almost another 100 years before Toyota released their mass-produced hybrid vehicle, the Prius.

Boys' toys What does the discerning billionaire buy when he wants to make a splash on the water? A yacht? A super-yacht? Try a "Giga-yacht." In 2009, Russian businessman Roman Abramovich launched *Eclipse*, the biggest private yacht in the world, costing an estimated $1.2 billion. Packed into its 557-ft (170-m) length—longer than five blue whales nose to tail—are two swimming pools (one of which converts into a dance floor), a movie theater, bulletproof windows, a mini submarine, a sophisticated missile defense system, and a laser system designed to seek out the cameras of floating paparazzi and destroy photographs before they can be taken! The sheer size of this Giga-yacht means that you could buy a Ferrari with the money it takes to fill it up with fuel, and once underway it costs an estimated $6,000 per hour to run at a top speed of 33 knots.

Cars taking part in the Le Mans 24-hour endurance race are 11 lb (5 kg) heavier at the end of the race than the start, due to dirt and splattered insects.

Lucky Larry who flew into LAX airport in a lawn chair
In 1982, Vietnam veteran and truck driver Larry Walters from California fulfilled a long-held dream and attached 42 helium weather balloons to his lawn chair. He expected to hover a leisurely 32 ft (10 m) off the ground, but the balloons were caught by the wind and surged to an incredible 16,000 ft (4,877 m). After drifting into the path of airliners landing at Los Angeles airport and becoming entangled in power lines, *Inspiration I*, as Larry christened his flying lawn chair, eventually touched the ground without injury. After a customary fine from the FAA, Larry became a celebrity overnight, appearing on *Letterman* and *The Tonight Show*.

Into the heavens Reverend Adelir Antonio de Carli from Brazil attached himself to 1,000 helium balloons in 2008 in an attempt to break a flight record. He was well equipped for the trip and reached a height of 20,000 ft (6,000 m), but unfortunately he was blown off course and the balloons were found in the ocean a few days later. His body was recovered shortly afterwards.

The black box flight recorder on airplanes is really orange.

Ghost yachts Echoing the story of the *Marie Celeste*, the catamaran *Kaz II* was found drifting 100 miles (160 km) off the coast of Queensland, Australia, in 2007—with no sign of its three-man crew. The engine and computers were running and a table had been laid for dinner, but the three sailors had seemingly vanished into thin air. In the absence of any bodies, the coroner concluded that the trio must have died in an unspecified freak accident.

Hot-air loons Hot-air ballooning seems like a peaceful, relaxing and not particularly dangerous activity, but for early balloonists the truth was somewhat different, as they generally used highly flammable hydrogen gas, instead of hot air or helium. In January 1785, the French inventor Jean-Pierre Blanchard and American John Jeffries used an early hydrogen gas balloon to make the first flight across the English Channel from the cliffs at Dover, England, towards Calais, France. At one point, the balloon descended to within a few hundred feet of the sea, forcing Blanchard and Jeffries to jettison all ballast and strip off their clothes before the balloon ascended again. Later that same year, Frenchman Jean-François Pilâtre de Rozier attempted to reverse Blanchard's channel journey. He had combined a hot-air balloon with a hydrogen balloon. This proved to be a bad decision, as sparks from the hot-air burner ignited the gas at 3,000 ft (914 m) and he became the first person to die in an air accident. Blanchard also pioneered the use of parachutes, throwing a dog attached to the new invention from one of his balloons. The dog survived, which paved the way for André-Jacques Garnerin to make the first successful, if violently uncomfortable, parachute drop to earth in 1797.

Most expensive cars

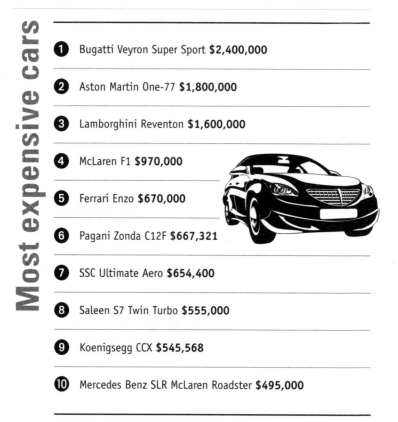

1 Bugatti Veyron Super Sport **$2,400,000**

2 Aston Martin One-77 **$1,800,000**

3 Lamborghini Reventon **$1,600,000**

4 McLaren F1 **$970,000**

5 Ferrari Enzo **$670,000**

6 Pagani Zonda C12F **$667,321**

7 SSC Ultimate Aero **$654,400**

8 Saleen S7 Twin Turbo **$555,000**

9 Koenigsegg CCX **$545,568**

10 Mercedes Benz SLR McLaren Roadster **$495,000**

Balloon Velocipede An Englishman by the name of Mr. Trinden hated falling off his bicycle and loathed cycling up hills. So, for his 1869 contraption, the "Balloon Velocipede," he attached his bicycle to a huge balloon, the idea being that the balloon's upward pull would fight gravity going up a hill and reduce his chances of falling off.

The Bugatti Veyron boasts a top speed of 267 mph (430 km/h), making it the fastest, legal streetcar It can achieve 0-60 mph (0-96 km/h) in just 2.6 seconds, but the commute to the office would not be cheap. The Veyron manages just 10 mpg (4.25 km/l) in city traffic. So in terms of fuel, a daily 40-mile (64-km) round trip would work out at $240 per week, or over $12,000 a year. Then there are the numerous other expenses—changing the tires (every 2,500 miles/ 4,000 km) amounts to about $25,300, and all four wheels have to be replaced every third tire change ($47,700). The first service costs round about $21,800—after that, the services get more expensive!

Half of the world's roundabouts are in France. There are over 30,000 of them.

Clyde Barrow, of Bonnie and Clyde fame, apparently wrote a "thank you" letter to Henry Ford for his Ford V8 getaway car It read: "I have drove Fords exclusively when I could get away with one. For sustained speed and freedom from trouble the Ford has got ever (sic) other car skinned and even if my business hasn't been strickly (sic) legal it don't hurt anything to tell you what a fine car you got in the V8." Barrow's love for the car couldn't prevent him from ultimately dying at the wheel of one, although his demise owed more to the hail of bullets delivered by a posse of Texas police officers than to any design faults in the V8.

Runaway train hero Mexican railroad engineer Jesús Garcia Corona became a national hero in 1907 when he drove a train loaded with dynamite away from the town of Nacozari to save the population perishing in the imminent explosion. Spotting that some hay on the roof of a car containing dynamite had caught fire, he drove the train at full steam nearly 4 miles (6 km) out of town before the dynamite exploded, killing him. In his honor, the town's name was changed to Nacozari de García.

The road that sings the *William Tell* Overture The world's grooviest road is surely a highway in Lancaster, California. A pattern of grooves has been cut into it so that it plays the *William Tell* Overture when driven on at 50 mph (80 km/h). Meanwhile, a road in Anyang, South Korea, keeps drivers awake by playing "Mary Had a Little Lamb."

Vehicle powered by dogs In 1880s' France, a Monsieur Huret invented a three-wheeled vehicle powered by dogs on treadmills positioned inside the two large, rear wheels. The idea was dropped following protests from animal-lovers.

FBI agent wrecks confiscated Ferrari Assigned to move a rare 1995 Ferrari F50 that had been recovered after being stolen from a dealer, FBI agent Fred Kingston managed to wreck it while negotiating a bend during a short drive in Kentucky. When the car's owner subsequently sued the U.S.

Justice Department for $750,000, it refused to pay, claiming that it was not liable for certain goods while they were in the hands of law enforcement.

Man accidentally ejects himself from plane As he soared through the sky in the back seat of a South African Air Force plane, a civilian passenger was intrigued to find out what the black-and-yellow-striped handle between his legs was for. So he pulled it—and was immediately blasted through the plane's Perspex canopy 330 ft (100 m) into space on his rocket-powered seat. He had inadvertently activated the eject lever. Happily, he was recovered unharmed.

The train for dead people The end of the line for thousands of Londoners in the late 19th and early 20th centuries was a railway dedicated to transporting corpses from the capital to Brookwood Cemetery in Surrey. The London Necropolis Railway opened in 1854, in response to chronic overcrowding in cemeteries where the same graves were being used over and over again for fresh internments, the previous occupants' bones often being left scattered on the ground or sold to local bone mills to be ground up as fertilizer. Two new stations were built on the line from London Waterloo—Brookwood South for Conformist burials and Brookwood North for non-Conformists. Mourners and deceased alike were divided into three classes, as was the custom on Britain's railways at the time. The dearly departed whose family had paid for them to travel first-class were treated with greater care, which explains why third-class mourners were not even allowed to watch the loading and unloading of their particular coffins. The funeral line was expected to prove highly profitable, but the opening of 32 new cemeteries hit business hard and by 1930 it was only operating one or two funeral trains a week. Ironically, the final nail in its coffin was the terrifying Blitz launched on London by the German Luftwaffe on the night of April 16, 1941, when over 1,000 Londoners were killed. Far from being good for trade, the bombing reduced the London Necropolis Railway to rubble. When the war ended, it was deemed too costly to rebuild.

Was the mass Toyota car recall caused by cosmic rays? When more than nine million Toyota cars were recalled in 2009 after sticky gas pedals caused sudden acceleration, experts were at a loss for an explanation. Then scientists came up with an intriguing theory—that the fault may have been the result of cosmic rays raining down on Earth. This radiation could have disrupted the microprocessors, software and memory chips of Toyota, a manufacturer that relied heavily on electronic controls in its cars. As the high-energy particles pass through electronic chips, they can cause a Single Event Upset (SEU) whereby a circuit may be reprogramed to carry out an unintended action.

Between 1983 and 2000, 53,487 people were involved in plane crashes in the United States, and 51,207 survived. Some 95% of air accidents have survivors.

The man who may have predicted the *Titanic* disaster
In 1886, British newspaper editor and spiritualist W.T. Stead published an article about the sinking of a liner in the Atlantic that resulted in huge loss of life due to a shortage of lifeboats. He warned, "This is exactly what might take place and will take place if liners are sent to sea short of boats." Six years later, he wrote a novel, *From the Old World to the New*, in which a ship sinks after colliding with an iceberg in the North Atlantic and the survivors are picked up by the White Star Line vessel, the *Majestic*. In April 1912, Stead himself embarked for the New World when President Taft invited him to address a peace conference in New York. Alas, he never arrived, having booked his passage on the White Star Line's newest liner, RMS *Titanic*.

When the *Titanic* hit the iceberg that sank the ship, the movie theater onboard was showing an early silent version of *The Poseidon Adventure*, in which a supposedly unsinkable ocean liner sinks.

The amusing story of Ireland's worst driver (who didn't exist) Irish police hunting the country's most reckless driver struggled to track down the suspect, a Mr. Prawo Jazdy, because whenever he was stopped, he gave a different address—over 50 in total. The serial offender was wanted everywhere from Cork to Cavan for speeding and parking violations until the realization dawned that Prawo Jazdy was Polish for "driving license" and not the first name and surname on the license.

Formula One auto shop bill A steering wheel costs $50,000, while tires cost $1,200 each and are designed to last a maximum of 125 miles (201 km). At this rate, the average driver would get through a set of tires every two weeks. Brakes cost more than $8,000 each, and don't last much more than 200 miles (320 km). If the average American took an F1 car to work every day, they would have spent around $125,000 on brakes by the end of the year.

Early car speed limits and regulations The 1865 Locomotive Act in the U.K. required all road locomotives, including cars, to travel at a maximum speed of 4 mph (6.4 km/h) in the country and 2 mph (3.2 km/h) in towns, and to have a crew of three, one of whom had to carry a red flag walking 60 yd (55 m) ahead to warn horse riders and horse-drawn traffic of the approach of a self-propelled vehicle. In 1890s' Pennsylvania, Quaker legislators passed a bill demanding that any drivers of horseless carriages must, upon encountering cattle or livestock, stop immediately, disassemble the automobile and "conceal the various components out of sight, behind nearby bushes" until the horses or livestock were sufficiently pacified. Fortunately, the State Governor vetoed the bill. The first driver stopped for speeding in the U.S. was New York cabbie Jacob

"maximum speed of 2 mph in towns"

German, who was jailed in 1899 for driving his electric taxi at the "breakneck speed" of 12 mph (19.3 km/h) on Lexington Avenue, where the speed limit was 8 mph (13 km/h).

Biplane powered by a steam boiler Built in 1933 by brothers George and William Besler and Nathan C. Price, the Tesla Air 2000 was a biplane powered by a steam boiler. It was promoted as being cheap (10 gal/38 l of water were enough for a flight of 400 miles/1,645 km), reliable and safe, as there was considerably less risk of fire than with conventional fuel. It was also so quiet that on the inaugural flight over California, spectators on the ground could hear the pilot calling to them. Alas, the Besler system proved unsuitable for larger planes.

The man who survived chopper blades In 1942, an executive at Bell Helicopters volunteered to test one of the earliest prototype production choppers. While hovering, he was pulled into the spinning rotor blades and flung some distance away from the copter. Amazingly, he survived, with only a broken arm.

Bill Gates' prohibited Porsche When Bill Gates and fellow Microsoft founder Paul Allen imported rare Porsche 959 sports cars to the United States in the 1980s, the cars were not permitted on U.S. roads because they had not been crash tested and were impounded for 13 years. So Microsoft engineers reportedly wrote software to create a crash simulation and help ensure the passage of legislation to let Gates, Allen and other wealthy owners such as Jerry Seinfeld drive their Porsches capable of 200 mph (321 km/h) on U.S. roads.

What happened to Amelia Earhart? The legendary pilot who vanished with her navigator Fred Noonan in 1937 while trying to fly around the world at the Equator may have survived as a castaway for months on a remote South Pacific island. A recent expedition to the uninhabited tropical island of Nikumaroro, where Earhart is believed to have landed when running out of fuel, found a campsite and nine separate fire features containing thousands of fish, turtle and bird bones, suggesting that many meals were eaten there. Other items recovered include cosmetic fragments of rouge from a woman's compact. The partial skeleton of what was thought to be a woman was found on the island in 1940, but the bones have since been lost. The remainder of the corpse was probably carried off by the thousands of ravenous crabs that inhabit the island.

Rescuing *Glacier Girl* After lying buried beneath nearly 300 ft (91 m) of snow and ice in Greenland for 50 years, a World War II fighter plane was excavated in a complex operation and restored to flying condition. The Lockheed P-38F Lightning, subsequently nicknamed *Glacier Girl*, was part of an eight-strong squadron flying across the Atlantic en route to Britain in June 1942. However, bad weather forced the squadron to make an emergency landing on an ice cap, and although the crews were rescued 10 days later, the planes were abandoned. Shifting ice, which carried *Glacier Girl* 2 miles (3.2 km) from her original location, and decades of snowfall prevented the plane from being located until 1988. Over the next four years, technicians obtained access by sinking long copper pipes filled with boiling water before using hot-water hoses to create a 50-ft-wide (15.3-m) operational chamber deep in the ice around the plane. They then took the plane apart and brought it to the surface, one piece at a time. Following painstaking reconstruction, *Glacier Girl* took to the skies again in 2002, a remarkable triumph over adversity.

***Spruce Goose*, the 1947 wooden plane that is still the biggest ever made (and flew only once)** Eccentric billionaire Howard Hughes ploughed $27 million into building a giant flying boat with a wingspan of 319 ft 11 in (97.5 m), the largest airplane ever constructed. Built entirely of wood because of the wartime restrictions on metals, it was nicknamed the *Spruce Goose*— but for Hughes this was one goose that never did lay a golden egg. Although commissioned in 1942 to

"largest plane ever made"

transport up to 700 troops as part of the U.S. war effort, it wasn't completed until two years after the war had ended. With its creator at the controls, *Spruce Goose* took off from the water in Long Beach Harbor on November 2, 1947, reached an altitude of 70 ft (21m), flew for about a mile (1.6 km) and landed—never to fly again. Its maiden—and only—flight had lasted just one minute. Ever hopeful of a second flight, Hughes retained a full crew to look after the giant plane in a special hangar right up until his death in 1976.

The world's longest train is the train transporting iron ore from Zouérate, Mauritania, to the coast at Nouadhibou. It is often 1.8 miles (3 km) long.

The fastest lap around Manhattan One Monday night in the summer of 2010, a group calling itself the Corporate Broadcasting Company circled the island of Manhattan in a Saturn Sky convertible in just 26 min 3 sec. That worked out at an average speed of 56 mph (90 km/h) for the 24.5-mile (39.4-km) run—not bad considering how many times they had to stop at traffic lights.

America's coast-to-coast king Erwin "Cannonball" Baker set an incredible 143 driving records over a period of 20 years. After starting off racing motorbikes against trains, he went on to specialize in U.S. coast-to-coast runs. In 1914, he rode from California to New York in 11.5 days—a whole nine days faster than the previous record—and this despite the fact that only four of his 3,379 miles (5,438 km) were on paved roads. Indeed, 68 miles (109 km) were actually on a railroad track. His most famous drive was a 1933 sprint from New York to Los

Angeles in a time that remained unsurpassed for nearly 40 years. His feats inspired the legendary Cannonball Run, subject of at least five movies and a TV series. Baker's old coast-to-coast records included:

- **1914 San Diego to New York by Indian motorcycle**
  11 days 11 hr 11 min
- **1915 L.A. to New York by Stutz Bearcat**
  11 days 7 hr 15 min
- **1916 L.A. to New York by Cadillac V8 Roadster**
  7 days 11 hr 52 min
- **1927 New York to San Francisco by 2-ton truck**
  5 days 17 hr 36 min
- **1928 New York to L.A. in a Franklin**
  2 days 21 hr 31 min
- **1933 New York to L.A. in a Graham-Paige Blue Streak 8**
  2 days 5 hr 30 min

From New York to L.A. in just over a day In October 2006, Alex Roy and codriver Dave Maher broke a 23-year record for the U.S. coast-to-coast run by blitzing from New York City to Santa Monica Pier, California, in just 31 hr 4 min. They covered the 2,800 miles (4,506 km) at an average speed of 90.1 mph (145 km/h) in a 2000 BMW M5. The run took place over Columbus Day weekend so as to meet minimal traffic and that enabled them to reach speeds of 160 mph (258 km/h) in places. Roy's route hit just four toll booths, three or four red lights, and one close call with highway patrol in Oklahoma.

Self-experimenting scientists

▪▪▫ *Australian doctor* **Barry Marshall** *won a Nobel Prize in 2005 after deliberately infecting himself with the bacterium that causes stomach ulcers.*

▪▪▫ *Researching hookworm infestation,* **Dr. Claude H. Barlow** *decided to eat adult intestinal worms drawn from the feces of infected patients in order to infect himself.*

▪▪▫ *In an attempt to confirm that mosquitoes transmitted yellow fever, U.S. physician* **Jesse William Lazear** *infected himself with yellow fever from mosquito bites without telling his colleagues. He died of the disease soon after.*

▪▪▫ *Aware that baboons are genetically close to humans but do not contract AIDS, in 1995 HIV-positive* **Jeff Getty** *infected his body with baboon bone marrow. The experiment failed as the baboon cells soon left his system, and he died in 2006.*

▪▪▫ *In 1928, Russian physician* **Alexander Bogdanov** *died following an experiment in which the blood of a student suffering from malaria and tuberculosis was given to him in a transfusion.*

▪▪▫ **Tim Friede** *immunizes himself against snake venom by allowing deadly mambas and cobras to bite him. One bite he received from a black mamba was so powerful that two of the fangs broke off in his hand.*

Why do men die before women? For years, men joked that it was nagging from women that drove them to an early grave. Now it appears that the supposed nagging from women may actually help prolong men's lives. On average, men die five years earlier than women, but experts believe that biological or genetic reasons account for just one year of the difference in life expectancy. The rest, they say, is due to men habitually refusing to go and see a doctor and therefore missing out on preventative health care. The American Psychological Association even suggests that the old joke about men being unable to survive without women may be true in matters of health. "Nagging from women," it writes, "is the main reason men ever get their health checked out."

The man who had a hole in his stomach In 1822, Canadian Alexis St. Martin was shot in the stomach, and the botched surgery he received left him with a gaping 6-in (15-cm) hole in his side. But it wasn't all bad news, as Dr. William Beaumont was able to discover the secrets of digestion by tying a silk string to pieces of beef, chicken, bread and cabbage and dangling them through the hole into St. Martin's stomach. Later pulling out the food, he found that vegetables took the longest to digest, chicken was digested more slowly than beef, and milk curdled before it could be digested.

Nobel Prize sperm bank In the late 1970s on an outbuilding of his Southern California estate, US tycoon and eugenicist

Robert K. Graham set up a sperm bank for Nobel Prize winners in a bid to reverse what he saw as the genetic decay all around him. By the time his repository closed in 1999, his "genius" sperm had created over 200 children.

Plague scientist dies of the plague Malcolm Casadaban, a plague researcher at the University of Chicago, died in 2009 from exposure to bacteria related to the plague.

The Sun makes up 99.8% of all the mass in our Solar System.

The woman who was dead for three hours In 1999, medical graduate Anna Bågenholm was skiing in Narvik, Norway, when she fell into a frozen stream, headfirst. She was pulled from the ice after 80 minutes, by which time her heart had stopped and her body temperature had dropped from 98.6°F (37°C) to just 56°F (13.7°C)—a body temperature at which nobody should survive. Bågenholm was airlifted to hospital where doctors experienced in hypothermia attempted to warm her blood. More than three hours after her heart stopped under the ice, it started to beat of its own accord—she was alive again. Her unprecedented low body temperature meant that her metabolism had slowed

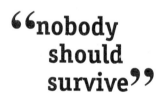
❝nobody should survive❞

by around 90%, and her brain needed far less oxygen than normal, protecting it from damage. To date, nobody has been "dead" for longer and survived.

The bacteria that create electricity In 1987, biologist Derek Lovley discovered a species of bacteria, *Geobacter metallireducens*, that can generate electricity. He and his team at the University of Massachusetts have even built microbial fuel cells powered by the bacteria with a view to creating a natural battery that could, one day, power sewage treatment plants.

Einstein was right: the higher you are, the faster you age Scientists have shown that one of Einstein's theories of relativity—that the further away from the Earth you are, the faster time passes—works even on a human scale. So, you will age faster if you live on the top floor of a skyscraper than if you live in a bungalow—but at a difference of just 104 millionths of a second over a 79-year lifespan, it's hardly going to matter.

The Chernobyl ghost city out of bounds for thousands of years Founded in 1970 to house workers from the Chernobyl Nuclear Power Plant, the Ukrainian city of Pripyat (population 50,000) was abandoned in 1986 following the disaster. Although radiation levels have dropped considerably and you can safely spend a day there, the city will remain uninhabitable for hundreds, probably thousands, of years.

Einstein's intelligence quiz

From the clues below, deduce who drinks water and who owns the zebra. It has been claimed that only 2% of the population can solve this quiz, attributed to iconic physicist Albert Einstein.

1 There are five houses in a row. Each is painted a different color, and their inhabitants are of different nationalities, they own different pets, drink different beverages and smoke different brands of cigarette.

2 The Englishman lives in the red house.

3 The Spaniard owns the dog.

4 Coffee is drunk in the green house.

5 The Ukrainian drinks tea.

6 The green house is immediately to the right of the ivory house.

7 The Old Gold smoker owns snails.

8 Kools are smoked in the yellow house.

9 Milk is drunk in the middle house.

10 The Norwegian lives in the first house.

11 The man who smokes Chesterfields lives in the house next to the man with the fox.

12 Kools are smoked in a house next to the house where the horse is kept.

13 The Lucky Strike smoker drinks orange juice.

14 The Japanese smokes Parliaments.

15 The Norwegian lives next to the blue house.

Solution to this quiz on page 254.

Vladimir P. Demikhov's two-headed dog experiment

Convinced that it would one day be possible to transplant human organs, Soviet surgeon Vladimir Demikhov tested his theory on dogs. One night in 1954, he took two dogs—one fully grown, the other a puppy—and stitched the head and upper body of the puppy to the mature German shepherd, connecting their blood vessels and windpipes. The resultant two-headed creature was like something out of science fiction, and journalists gasped as both heads simultaneously lapped at bowls of milk—and then winced as the milk from the puppy's head dribbled from the unconnected stump of its esophageal tube. Even for the science-crazy 1950s, this was hard to stomach, which was probably why Demikhov didn't receive much praise outside Russia for an experiment that predated the first human heart transplant by 13 years. The animals died shortly afterward from tissue rejection, but that didn't stop Demikhov creating 19 more two-headed dogs over the following years.

The real first man in space The first man in space wasn't a Russian astronaut; it was American test pilot Joseph Kittinger at the height of the space race between the two superpowers. In 1960, he was assigned to discover whether an astronaut could survive an aborted mission, even 20 miles (32 km) above the Earth. Kittinger took off from New Mexico attached to a large balloon. He took one hour and 43 minutes to ascend to 102,800 ft (31,330 m), where temperatures can drop as low as −148°F (−100°C). After six minutes on the edge of space, he jumped off his platform.

"20 miles above the Earth"

The average Cessna light aircraft can only fly to 13,500 ft (4,115 m), and even Concorde topped out at 60,000 ft (18,288 m). Kittinger was so high up that initially he felt no wind resistance. He fell for 4 min 36 sec, reaching a blistering maximum speed of 614 mph (988 km/h), before opening his parachute at 18,000 ft (5,500 m). From his vantage point in the heavens, Kittinger radioed down to earth that he had a "hostile sky above... man may live in space, but he will never conquer it." In 2008, the French skydiver Michel Fournier was due to attempt to break Kittinger's record, but when his $200,000 balloon was inflated on the ground, it flew off into the sky without him and ended his dream for the foreseeable future.

Will the Large Hadron Collider destroy itself in the future? Two eminent scientists have voiced the fear that the elusive Higgs boson particle, which physicists hope to produce by banging protons together in the Large Hadron Collider beneath Switzerland, might be so abhorrent to nature that its creation would actually dart backward through time and stop the Collider before it could make one. *The New York Times* described the hypothesis as being "like a time traveler who goes back in time to kill his grandfather."

And you thought Everest was tall...

The Moon	Mons Huygens	*15,420 ft / 4,700 m*
Earth	Mount Everest	*29,028 ft / 8,848 m*
Venus	Maxwell Montes	*36,089 ft / 11,000 m*
Io (moon of Jupiter)	Boösaule Montes	*55,774 ft / 17,000 m*
Iapetus (moon of Saturn)	Equatorial ridge	*65,616 ft / 20,000 m*
Mars	Olympus Mons	*69,458 ft / 21,171 m*

Tallest mountains

Mini black holes on Earth You always think of black holes as being in the depths of space, but they might be closer to home than you realize. Recent research has shown that miniature black holes may even be passing through Earth every day. But don't worry about being swallowed up by one—these mini black holes are harmless and are smaller than atoms.

Moon landings faked, Bangladesh claims Two Bangladeshi newspapers had to apologize after publishing an article taken from satirical U.S. website *The Onion*, which claimed the Moon landings were faked. They reported that Neil Armstrong had told a shocked news conference that he now knew the landings had been an "elaborate hoax." Neither newspaper realized that *The Onion* was not a genuine news site.

The coldest temperature ever created In 2009, scientists in Helsinki, Finland, used magnetic refrigeration to cool the metal rhodium to 100pK—or, rather, 0.000,000,000,1 degrees above absolute zero, which is −459.67°F (−273°C)—the coldest temperature ever recorded and over one trillion times colder than liquid nitrogen.

Could poison gas save our lives? Just an ounce of poison gas—hydrogen sulfide—is enough to kill dozens of people. But U.S. biologist Mark Roth believes he has found a way to utilize it to save lives. Death isn't caused by oxygen deprivation as such, but by a chain of damaging chemical reactions triggered by sharply dropping oxygen levels. Those reactions require the presence of oxygen, so when it is replaced by hydrogen sulfide, the reaction doesn't occur and the patient lives on. With rats and mice, Roth can administer a seemingly fatal dose of hydrogen sulfide but the animal merely enters a state of suspended animation, and within minutes of inhaling ordinary air, it is scurrying around again as if nothing had happened. Whether it will work on humans remains to be seen.

How to dip your hand in boiling oil, liquid nitrogen and molten lead without losing it The Leidenfrost Effect is a phenomenon that creates a tiny boundary to protect your skin at extreme temperatures. For example, if you dip wet fingers into molten lead, the heat from the lead focuses on evaporating the water, not burning your hand, and the resultant layer of steam actually insulates your hand, sparing you pain. Be warned, though—the effect doesn't last for long, so it's best not to chance it.

Sir Charles Blagden's 270°F (132°C) human oven experiment To study the role of perspiration in the thermoregulation of the body, 18th-century British physician Sir Charles Blagden spent eight minutes in a room that had been heated to 270°F (132°C). For protection against the inferno, on top of his ordinary clothes he wore a pair of thick worsted stockings pulled up over his shoes to above his knees, a pair of gloves, and he held a cloth to his face. Despite water boiling in pots and eggs and steak becoming "rather overdone" in the room, Blagden reported feeling no great discomfort, though his pulse was beating at double its normal rate.

❚ ❙ ❙

Crazy psychiatrist Dr. Henry Cotton, who would remove your organs to make you sane Henry Aloysius Cotton, a psychiatrist at the New Jersey State Hospital in the 1920s, did not adhere to conventional means of treating mental illness. He had no time for the Freudian theory that such disorders stemmed from childhood traumas. Instead, he was convinced that the root of all evil lay in pus. Cotton argued that depression, hallucinations and all other mania were the result of nasty old pus spreading infections through the body. His solution was simple—remove the source of the problem. He began with decaying teeth,

❝ the root of all evil lay in pus ❞

extracting thousands of teeth from patients every year, and when their mental problems stubbornly refused to be cured overnight, he started on their organs. Tonsils, sinuses, spleens, stomachs and cervixes were all removed in the hope that the patient would be cured of madness. By the time he dropped dead of a heart attack in 1933, hundreds of patients had died and thousands had been maimed by Cotton's methods. Nobody had realized that he was even crazier than his patients.

You don't know the back of your hand as well as you thought A recent scientific study indicates that our brains grossly misrepresent the size and shape of our own hands. Volunteers were asked to place their left hand palm-down on a table, and when the hand was then covered with a board, they were told to mark on the board where they thought their fingertips and knuckles were. The data was then used to reconstruct the brain's image of the hand. The results showed that we think of our hands as being considerably shorter and fatter than they really are. This misjudgement by the brain may not be solely confined to the hands, and may have implications in the study of eating disorders.

Why do astronauts' bones shrink? Astronauts who spend a long time in space can lose up to 2% of their bone mass each month due to the effects of prolonged weightlessness on the human body. Our bones constantly reshape themselves in response to the stresses placed on them, but in space they no longer have to fight against gravity, and so less strain is exerted on the skeletal system. This reduced level of stress means that while old bone continues to be removed, new bone is not being built, resulting in shrinkage, particularly in the lower half of the body.

The 10,000-mile toilet flush Once a year, up to 11 tons of human waste from Antarctic bases are shipped all the way to a landfill in California.

Mad Victorian medicine

Oil of earthworms, opium and cannabis cough mixture were just some of the remedies available from the Victorian chemist.

▪▪▪ Between 1890 and 1910, **heroin** was sold as a nonaddictive substitute for morphine. It was also used to treat children with a bad cough.

▪▪▪ **Cocaine** drops were a popular cure for children with toothache.

▪▪▪ **Opium** was the painkiller of choice in Victorian Britain, particularly for pacifying babies.

▪▪▪ **Dr. Batty's Asthma Cigarettes** were smoked by 19th-century Americans to treat asthma, hay fever, foul breath, head colds and all diseases of the throat.

▪▪▪ **Oil of earthworms** (prepared by boiling dried earthworms in olive oil and wine) was rubbed into the skin to relieve muscular pain.

▪▪▪ **46% alcohol** was used to treat babies who were teething.

▪▪▪ A bottle of **cannabis** in 74% alcohol was an effective medicine in the U.S.

▪▪▪ Victorian women used **poisonous belladonna** as a beauty aid.

■■■ *Cough mixtures of the period often contained both* **opium and cannabis.**

■■■ *The Victorians used* **toxic arsenic** *to deal with all manner of ailments from malaria to rheumatism. It was also used to treat morning sickness, despite its acknowledged side effect of causing extreme vomiting.*

Why is the sky blue? The Earth's atmosphere is mostly composed of nitrogen and oxygen. Sunlight is made up of all the colors of the rainbow, and as it fights its way through air molecules, blue light is reflected the most efficiently. So that is what our eyes see. However, for the first two billion years of Earth's history, the sky was probably orange as the atmosphere's primary component then was methane.

Jupiter is so big because it once swallowed a planet
It seems that the reason Jupiter is the biggest planet in the Solar System—more than 120 times the size of Earth—is because it once gobbled up a smaller rival. Scientists believe Jupiter crashed into a planet that was about ten times the size of Earth and was on its way to becoming a gas giant itself. The incoming rocky planet was flattened as it hit Jupiter's atmosphere and quickly hit Jupiter's core, causing it to vaporize. They say the collision explains why Jupiter has such a small core in relation to its size.

The Russian who put his head in a particle accelerator and survived The Earth's atmosphere is mostly composed of nitrogen and on July 13, 1978, Anatoli Bugorski was checking a component of the U-70 synchrotron particle accelerator when he accidentally put his head in the beam's path, instantly exposing himself to a dose of radiation hundreds of times more powerful than one which is normally fatal. He reported seeing a flash "brighter than a thousand suns" as protons traveling at around the speed of light shot through the left side of his head. Although he experienced no pain, that side of his face quickly swelled alarmingly, and over the next few days his skin peeled off to reveal the exact path the proton beam had carved through his skull. Everyone expected him to die, but against all the odds he pulled through with nothing worse than a paralyzed left side of the face, loss of hearing and increased fatigue. In fact, he even went on to complete his PhD. Bugorski's survival was a demonstration—albeit unintentional and on a considerably larger scale—of radiotherapy. Being 2,000 times heavier than electrons, protons don't dissipate much when they hit the body, and so when passing through his head the narrow beam did not affect surrounding areas such as the brain. It is the same localized power that doctors harness that spared Bugorski's life.

❝protons shot through the left side of his head❞

Marie Curie's radioactive papers More than a century after her pioneering work on radioactivity, Marie Curie's scientific papers are still radioactive. As a result, they are stored in lead-lined boxes in France's Bibliotheque National, and anyone wishing to view them must do so wearing protective clothing—and even then only after signing a waiver of liability. Curie and her husband Pierre were, of course, blissfully ignorant of the dangers of radiation, which eventually led to her death in 1934. She would merrily carry bottles of polonium and radium in her coat pocket and store them in her desk drawer, remarking on the pretty blue-green light that the substances gave off in the dark. Consequently her furniture, too, remains contaminated to this day. Your chances of ever seeing her papers without a chemical suit are pretty slim as the most common isotope of radium—radium-226—has a half-life of 1,600 years.

The corpse farm in Tennessee A two-acre area of East Tennessee, known as the "Body Farm," is littered with human corpses to help real-life crime scene investigators learn the correct way to dig up a buried body. Established in 1971 by forensic anthropologist Dr. Bill Bass, the farm receives up to 50 donated bodies a year, which are scattered around the facility and exposed in different ways—clothed, unclothed, in sun, shade, water, and trunks of cars—so that decomposition can be studied under varying conditions. CSI teams attend courses there, learning such techniques as identifying the time of death through the presence of maggots. Dr. Bass says the unit has "solved a lot of crimes, and put some bad people in prison."

The four-year-old marathon runner In 2006, Budhia Singh, a four-year-old boy from the slums of Bhubaneshwar, India, ran 40 miles (64 km) nonstop along country roads in just over seven hours in temperatures of 90°F (32°C). He had been running marathons since the age of three but this was his crowning achievement. Some hailed him as "Marathon Boy," but others were concerned that one so young was being exploited for financial gain, and a week later Orissa state authorities banned him from running marathons again until the age of 11. Controversy surrounded his coach, Biranchi Das, who had trained him to run huge distances on a daily basis, and the following year Das was arrested on suspicion of torturing the boy. Budhia Singh showed reporters scars that he claimed were the result of the coach's mistreatment. "He hung me upside down from a ceiling fan," he said. "He beat me with a hot iron rod and locked me in a room for two days without food." Das vigorously denied the accusations and after a full medical examination of the boy, all charges were dropped. Then, in 2008, Das was shot dead following a training session at a judo center. Two men were subsequently convicted of the killing.

The Olympic champion gymnast who had a wooden leg George Eyser had his left leg amputated after being run over by a train, but that didn't stop him from representing the U.S. at the 1904 St. Louis Olympics—with a wooden leg. What's more, he went on to win six medals, including three gold—on the long horse vault, the parallel bars and the rope climb.

An Olympic gold medal is almost 99% silver.

The sauna sportsmen who cooked themselves In 2010, the sauna world championships in Finland came to an inevitable end. As the competition heated up, the field was thinned to two sauna athletes, Russian contestant Vladimir Ladyzhenskiy and five-time champion Timo Kaukonen from Finland. As temperatures inside the sauna soared to 230°F (110°C)—slow cooking in a family oven—Kaukonen began to show signs of discomfort and organizers pulled him out. Ladyzhenskiy followed, only to collapse outside. After seven minutes in such intense heat they had literally begun to cook, with scalded skin sliding off their flesh, and both were rushed to the hospital. Ladyzhenskiy was pronounced dead shortly afterwards, while Kaukonen was badly burned and fell into a coma from which he awoke after two months. His verdict? "I should have quit earlier." Putting their lives on the line did not bring them glory. As neither of the men had left the sauna of their own accord, the championship was awarded to Finnish competitor lkka Pöyhiä, who had already vacated the human oven safely. At the time of writing, the future of the Sauna World Championships was in doubt.

The U.S. are the reigning Olympic Rugby Union champions That's because they won gold by beating France 17–3 in Paris in 1924, the last time that rugby was an Olympic sport. The French crowd were so angry that at the final whistle they hurled bottles and rocks and one of the American reserves was hit in the face by a walking stick.

The ancient South American ballgame—with skulls for balls and both the winners and losers sacrificed The "Mesoamerican ballgame," played by pre-Columbian peoples such as the Aztecs, must rank as the most violent sport ever invented. The game itself was an aggressive affair, something like volleyball, but getting a heavy rubber ball in the face was nothing compared to the fate of some of the players, who were ritually sacrificed after the game—winners and losers! There is evidence that some codes of the sport ramped up the gore, swapping the regular balls for the decapitated skulls of the sacrificed. At Tula, in Mexico, a large skull rack, or *tzompantli*, stood on the ballcourt ready for unfortunate athletes.

Will smoking vulture brains make your gambling picks any more reliable? A South African medicinal practice known as *muti* involves smoking vulture brains, which supposedly give the user a clearer vision of the future. The brains are dried, ground up and then smoked in cigarettes. A tiny vial of vulture brains sells for around $6.50.

The pigeon-shooting event at the 1900 Olympics used live birds, and 300 were killed.

Accidental record breaker In 2008, Norwegian skier Fred Syversen accidentally broke the skiing cliff drop world record by almost 100 ft (30.5 m) after he flew off the edge of a 350-ft (107-m) cliff in the Alps and was buried in the snow below. Despite leaving the mountain at 50 mph (80 km/h) and plummeting the equivalent of 30 stories, Syversen escaped serious injury. Jamie Pierre from the United States was presumably not happy that his (intentional) record, set the year before, had been broken by accident.

The billion-mile golf drive Eat your heart out, Tiger Woods! In 2006, Russian cosmonaut Mikhail Tyurin drove a golf ball a billion miles. Using a gold-plated six iron, he launched the ball into orbit from a special tee attached to a platform on the International Space Station 220 miles (355 km) above Earth. The ball was expected to circle the Earth for up to four years at a speed of 5 miles (8 km) per second before falling from orbit and burning up in the atmosphere.

Mountaineer becomes second to tweet from the top of Everest (but thought he was the first) In May 2011, Britain's Kenton Cool claimed to be the first man to have tweeted from the summit of Mount Everest—unaware that American polar explorer Eric Larsen had beaten him to it by about six months. Still, Cool did have the consolation of being the first person to make a 3G phone call from Everest, when he rang his wife from the summit.

Bizarre sports

■■■ **Fox tossing** *In this barbaric 18th-century European sport, a team of two people used a long canvas sling to propel a live fox as high into the air as possible—up to 25 ft (7.5 m) with practice. The game was over when all the foxes were dead. Even ladies of the court played it.*

■■■ **Octopus wrestling** *A diver fought a large octopus in shallow water and dragged it to the surface. The sport was so popular in the 1960s that the annual World Octopus Wrestling Championship was shown on U.S. TV.*

■■■ **Sheep counting** *Hundreds of sheep run across a field in Australia while competitors do their best to count them without falling asleep.*

■■■ **Toilet racing** *In Canada's Great Klondike Outhouse Race, teams wheel outdoor toilets around a 1.5-mile (2.4-km) course. One person must sit on the toilet throughout the race.*

■■■ **Buzkashi** *Afghanistan's national sport is a team game played on horseback—a bit like polo but with the carcass of a headless goat for a ball.*

■■■ **Dwarf tossing** *Competitors hurl dwarfs wearing padded clothing or Velcro costumes onto mattresses or Velcro-coated walls. Banned in many countries.*

■■■ **Wife carrying** *At the annual Wife-Carrying World Championships in Finland, runners carry their wives across an obstacle course, the winner receiving his wife's weight in beer.*

The footballer who ran the wrong way Roy Riegels earned his place in American Football folklore as a result of a highly individual move in the 1929 Rose Bowl. Playing at center for the California Golden Bears, Riegels collected a fumble from opponents Georgia Tech on their 20-yd line and sprinted off on an electrifying run. The 53,000-strong crowd rose in unison. They had never seen anything like it before—Riegels was running in the wrong direction, towards his own goal! Finally, just a yard short of his own line, Riegels was brought to earth by a tackle from teammate Benny Lom. Riegels' brainstorm enabled Georgia to pick up two decisive points toward a narrow 8-7 win. Riegels, who said afterward that he thought the shouts from the crowd were yells of encouragement, became an unlikely hero. He received a mountain of fan mail, including a proposal of marriage in which he and his bride would walk up the aisle instead of down.

All 11 members of a soccer team were killed by lightning during a match in the Democratic Republic of the Congo on October 25, 1998. The other team was untouched.

Marathons are bad for you All this talk about running being healthy may be wide of the mark. Three competitors died of heart attacks during the 2009 Detroit half-marathon, and don't forget that the same fate befell 52-year-old Jim Fixx, the man who boasted about the health benefits of jogging. Perhaps there's something to be said for being a couch potato.

▪▪▪ **The first person to go over the Niagara Falls and survive** *was a woman. Annie Taylor—a 63-year-old schoolteacher from Michigan—took the plunge in a barrel in 1901, emerging uninjured save for a small gash to the head.*

▪▪▪ **An English stuntman, Bobby Leach, tackled the Falls in a steel barrel** *in 1911. He survived—but spent the next six months in hospital to repair his broken bones. Ironically, he died in 1926, after slipping on an orange peel and breaking his leg on a New Zealand street.*

▪▪▪ **Charles Stephens, a 58-year-old English barber and father of 11, plunged over the Horseshoe Falls in an oak barrel** *in 1920. There were straps inside for his arms, and he secured an anvil to his feet for ballast. When the barrel hit the base of the falls, the anvil crashed through the bottom of it carrying him to his death.*

▪▪▪ **Greek-born American George A. Stathakis went over the falls in a huge wood and steel barrel** *in 1930, along with his pet turtle, Sonny. The barrel was hardly damaged in the drop but was then stuck behind the falls for 20 hours and by the time it was retrieved, poor George had died of suffocation. Sonny, believed to be 150 years old, miraculously survived.*

▪▪▪ **In 1951, Red Hill Jr. rode over the falls in a homemade contraption** *consisting of 14 rubber truck-tire inner tubes* *covered with heavy canvas and held together with a thick net. When it was recovered, Hill's vessel had been ripped to shreds, and the only evidence of its occupant was a pair of shoes. The next day his battered body was pulled from the Niagara River.*

▪▪▪ **Aspiring U.S. stuntman Jessie W. Sharp attempted to ride the falls in a kayak** *in 1990—without safety helmet or life jacket. So confident was he of succeeding that he made dinner reservations for that evening. His body has never been recovered.*

▪▪▪ **Californian Robert Overacker went over the Canadian Horseshoe Falls on a single jet ski** *in 1995, but the rocket-propelled parachute on his back failed to discharge and he died on impact with the water.*

U.S. tennis player Venus Williams was docked a point at the 1999 Australian Open Championships after a string of beads dislodged from her dreadlocked hair and scattered around the court.

Japan's useless hole-digging competition Each year thousands of competitors flock to the outskirts of Tokyo to take part in Japan's National Hole Digging Competition. Working in teams, shovels in hands, contestants have 30 minutes to dig as deep a hole as possible. Points are also awarded for the most creative holes and for wearing unusual costumes, the winner taking home $1,200 and the coveted "Golden Shovel" trophy. At the end of the contest, all the holes (creative or not) are filled in, ready to be started again next year.

The soccer goal celebration that cost a player his finger Playing for Swiss club Servette in 2004, Paulo Diogo helped set up a goal and celebrated by jumping up on the metal perimeter fence. Alas, he forgot that he was wearing his wedding ring (he had only recently got married) and it caught in the barrier. As he jumped off the fence, most of his finger was ripped off along with the ring. To add insult to injury, the referee booked him for time wasting during his celebration, when in fact stewards were frantically searching for his missing finger.

Demonstration sports at the 1900 Paris Olympics included kite flying, firefighting and lifesaving.

How casinos help you to lose more money Casinos are meticulously designed to help relieve you of your loose change. There are no clocks, no windows, floors slope towards the middle of the gaming room, and all the theaters and bathrooms are way past the games and machines. The gaudy, vibrant carpets are part of the way in which casinos stimulate your senses, keeping you awake, and helping to disorient you. There are no obvious pathways on the floor, meaning people navigate toward the machines. The exits out into the world are hard to see from the gambling floor—you cannot see very far into the casino without physically exploring the room, like a maze. The sounds of most casino machines are all in the key of C major, a happy sounding key (as opposed to D minor for example), so the background noise is not unpleasant for the gambler. The machines that pay out the most are situated where customers have to walk, the sounds of winning enticing them toward the main clusters of machines, which do not pay out as easily. Although it is a myth that casinos pipe in oxygen to keep gamblers alert, they perfume the air, which has been proved to increase revenue by up to 50%. Classic casino colors are red and gold, with gold related to wealth while red, which we are hardwired to associate with danger, stimulates us and encourages us to make quick decisions and take risks. In this environment people spend more money.

The world's strongest man? Born and raised in Brooklyn, New York, Joe Rollino stood only 5 ft 5 in (1.7 m) tall and weighed just 150 lb (68 kg), but in the 1920s he was able to lift more than 20 times his body weight with his back. He bent nails with his mouth, coins with his bare hands, and once lifted 635 lb (288 kg) with one finger. On another occasion, he lifted 475 lb (215 kg) with his teeth. He appeared as a strongman at the Coney Island Festival and later worked as a bodyguard for Greta Garbo. Interestingly for someone associated with raw strength, Rollino was a lifelong vegetarian. His fitness regime helped him live to 104, and even then his 2010 death was the result of a road traffic accident.

Sporting frauds

▪▪▪ *Cuban-American* **Rosie Ruiz** *collapsed dramatically over the line as she was declared the surprise winner of the 1980 Boston Marathon. Yet she hadn't even run the race, having jumped out of the crowd a mile from the finish. She had qualified for Boston after apparently finishing 11th in the New York Marathon—but it later transpired that she had taken the subway for most of that route.*

▪▪▪ *Milwaukee postman* **Walter Danecki** *lied that he was a professional golfer so that he could join the qualifiers at the 1965 British Open. His cover was blown after he posted scores of 108 and 113 to finish 81 over par.*

▪▪▪ *Baseball prodigy* **Danny Almonte** *was supposedly just 12 years old when he became a Little League sensation pitching for the Bronx Baby Boomers in 2001. When it was revealed that he was really 14, the Boomers were stripped of their title.*

▪▪▪ *In 1990, U.S. jockey* **Sylvester Carmouche** *shocked punters at Louisiana's Delta Downs racetrack by romping home on 23-1 outsider Landing Officer. However, he was banned for ten years when it emerged that shortly after the start he had hidden his horse in thick fog and waited for the rest of the runners to complete a circuit of the track before rejoining the race.*

▪▫▪ *Polish-American athlete* **Stanislawa Walasiewicz** *(also known as Stella Walsh) won gold in the women's 100 meters at the 1932 Olympics. In 1980, as an innocent bystander, she was shot dead during a botched robbery in Cleveland—and her autopsy showed that she had male genitalia.*

The 64-year-old who kayaked across the Atlantic on his own Aleksander Doba from Poland kayaked nonstop across the Atlantic in 2011—a distance of 3,320 miles (5,312 km). Almost 99 days after leaving Dakar in Senegal, Doba arrived in Brazil with his kayak, which measured 23 ft (7 m) in length. The first thing he asked for was a beer.

In chess, "checkmate" derives from the Persian phrase *shah mat*, **meaning "the king is dead."**

Ice hockey goaltender came within 0.1 in (3 mm) of death Canadian Clint Malarchuk was tending goal for Buffalo Sabres in 1989 when he was cut on the neck by the skating blade of St. Louis Blues' Steve Tuttle, severing his internal carotid artery. As pools of blood stained the ice, the team's trainer, Jim Pizzutelli, reached into Malarchuk's neck and stemmed the bleeding until doctors arrived. They said that if the skate had hit Malarchuk's jugular just 0.1 in (3 mm) higher, he would have been dead within two minutes.

The man in the iron mask For a century it was believed that in 1908 English adventurer Harry Bensley, wearing an iron mask and pushing a pram, had set off from London on a six-year trek to win a $100,000 bet with eccentric American millionaire J. Pierpont Morgan that he could walk around the world without being identified. The terms of the wager stipulated that Bensley had to visit 169 British towns, followed by 125 cities in 18 other countries, in the course of which he also had to find himself a wife—no mean feat since she, too, was not permitted to see his face. He set off with £1 to his name and a change of underwear in the pram. According to Bensley, by 1914 he had visited 12 countries—including the U.S.A., Canada, Australia, China and Japan—and had received 200 offers of marriage, all of which he had declined, before the outbreak of World War I forced him to cancel the bet in Italy. However, there is now genuine doubt that he ever left Britain as his family can find no evidence of him venturing abroad and certainly none of newfound wealth. For even if he had been paid just one-fifth of the money, as was suggested, he would have been a very rich man, picking up the equivalent of $400,000 today. It seems that when Bensley died in 1956, he took his secret to the grave.

The fraudster set free to play poker in order to pay back his victims Convicted of stealing nearly $450,000 from 23 investors over several years, former insurance agent Samuel McMaster Jr., of Albuquerque, New Mexico, offered to repay his victims through poker winnings. Prosecutors agreed to the unusual request, and sentencing was postponed to give McMaster the chance to win enough money to wipe the slate clean. There the fairy tale ended. For his luck ran out at the poker table and he was sentenced to 12 years in prison.

World Trade Center tightrope walker Back in the 1970s, French high-wire artist Philippe Petit spent over six years planning a daring walk between the Twin Towers of the World Trade Center, a quarter of a mile above the streets of Manhattan. Using fake ID cards, Petit and his collaborators posed as construction workers to gain access to the building as part of the lengthy preparation for what he called the "artistic crime of the century." He used secretly taken photographs to build a model of the towers so that he knew what equipment would be needed for the walk. Finally on the night

❝walking a quarter of a mile above❞ Manhattan

of August 6–7, 1974, he and his crew rode in an elevator to the 104th floor and, using a bow and arrow, rigged a 450-lb (205-kg) steel cable across the 200-ft (60-m) gap. At 7.15 a.m. Petit stepped off the South Tower and began a 45-minute walk, crossing the wire eight times, even pausing to sit on it, lie on it, dance on it and make knee salutes. Witnesses on the ground could only watch his antics in wonderment. As rain started to fall, the police arrested him, but all charges against him were dropped. Instead, the owners of the WTC were so delighted by the positive publicity that they offered him a lifetime pass to the observation deck and asked him to sign a steel beam close to where he had started his death-defying walk.

▪ ▪ ▪

The epic treasure hunt from beyond the grave When Patty Henken bought an antique chair at an auction in 2008, she found a typewritten note signed by "Chauncey Wolcott" stating that she would find a chest containing $250 in U.S. gold coins buried 12 ft (3.6 m) below ground in the yard of a house in Springfield, Illinois. She and her husband hired a mechanical excavator to dig up the vacant lot, but found nothing more valuable than bricks and bottles... along with the realization that they had been the latest victims of a notorious prankster who died more than 30 years earlier. For when Betty Atkinson Ryan of Mason City, Iowa, read about the Henkens' treasure hunt, she immediately thought of her old boss, John "Jay" Slaven, an incorrigible hoaxer who often used the name "Chauncey Wolcott" and who lived for decades at the location of the dig. He also had a penchant for composing his jokes on a typewriter. Slaven died in 1976, but, as the Henkens can sadly testify, he had one last laugh up his sleeve.

▪ ▪ ▪

After each fight, Ukrainian world heavyweight boxing champion Vitali Klitschko keeps his fists from swelling by wrapping them in his young son Max's urine-soaked diapers.

The gambler who broke Monte Carlo Nineteenth-century Yorkshire engineer Joseph Jagger had long devoted his energies to the workings of the roulette wheel, and observed that, instead of being purely random selections, the winning numbers were often the result of mechanical imbalances. In 1873, he hired six assistants to monitor the outcomes of six roulette wheels at the

"collected nearly $5 million"

Beaux-Arts Casino in Monte Carlo and found that on one of the wheels, nine numbers (7, 8, 9, 17, 18, 19, 22, 28 and 29) came up more frequently than the others. Two years later, on July 7, 1875, he used his inside knowledge to win over $1 million in today's money. Over the next three days, he and fellow gamblers who followed his lead collected the modern equivalent of nearly $5 million. The casino retaliated by switching the wheels, but after a losing streak, Jagger spotted a telltale scratch on his original wheel and immediately returned to his winning ways. The casino responded by daily moving the frets—the metal dividers between numbers—and Jagger eventually gave up. Even so, he left Monte Carlo with his two million francs ($5 million in 2011) and never returned. Back in the U.K., he resigned from his job and invested his money in property.

A game of international Ping-Pong made it possible for President Nixon to make the first ever, American diplomatic visit to the People's Republic of China.

Richest men ever to have lived

1 **John D. Rockefeller**
U.S. oil baron *$336 billion*

2 **Andrew Carnegie**
U.S. steel magnate *$309 billion*

3 **William the Conqueror**
11th-century English king *$209 billion*

4 **Cornelius Vanderbilt**
U.S. railroad entrepreneur *$185 billion*

5 **Alan Rufus**
11th-century Norman nobleman *$149 billion*

6 **Bill Gates**
U.S. computer guru *$136 billion*

7 **William de Warenne**
11th-century Norman nobleman *$134 billion*

8 **John Jacob Astor**
U.S. real estate investor *$121 billion*

9 **Richard Fitzalan**
10th Earl of Arundel, 14th-century
English nobleman *$108 billion*

10 **Stephen Girard**
18th-century Franco-American merchant *$105 billion*

Note: all figures adjusted to present-day values

Before Madoff: the original Ponzi Scheme When Wall Street financier Bernard Madoff made off with billions of dollars invested in his front company by hundreds of individuals and corporations, it was called the biggest "Ponzi scheme" in history. The original Ponzi would have been proud of Madoff's efforts. Charles Ponzi was born in Parma, Italy, in 1882 and moved to the United States in November 1903. He worked low-paid jobs for 14 years as he traveled around different cities. In Montreal, he found himself in prison after forging a signature on a blank check he had come across while on a job hunt. After a further spell in an Atlanta jail for people smuggling, he came up with his most infamous scam, in Boston. Ponzi realized that the system by which Americans could send postal coupons abroad, and vice versa, had a loophole. By trading cheap foreign postal stamps against a stronger U.S. dollar, he could make a large profit on each small transaction. He soon began raking in investors, and while he did pay the first batch of speculators, he began to pay out returns from the money given to him by new investors—the classic Ponzi scheme as we know it today. Most investors would reinvest the returns, so he didn't have to pay out, and he was running at a loss.

At the height of the Ponzi frenzy, he was raking in the modern equivalent of $2.5 million every day, money with which he had effectively bought a bank in Boston. Ponzi was so arrogant that he sued *The Boston Post* for $500,000 for questioning his finances, and won. The paper got their revenge not long after, however, by publishing details of Ponzi's postal scheme, which laid bare the fact that there was no way that the postal coupons could underpin the money going through

Ponzi's hands, with only 0.02% of the required coupons in circulation. The paper worked out that even if Ponzi had sent out all the postal coupons, the overheads would have wiped out the profits. His scheme was completely unviable yet attracted millions and millions of dollars.

Ponzi deflected criticism of his scheme when he assured a crowd of angry investors at his office by personally giving out two million dollars in a couple of days, plus coffee and donuts. He was so convincing that many left their money with him. However, the adverse publicity attracted a serious investigation, which would be the end of him. By the time Ponzi was foiled, despite the huge amounts of cash he was handling, he was found to be $7 million dollars in debt, the equivalent of $75 million in today's money.

Even as he was being investigated for the postal fraud, the irrepressible Ponzi devised another scam while on bail, selling swampland in Florida. He eventually died penniless in a Brazilian charity hospital in 1949. In his last interview, from the hospital, he finally admitted his Boston postal scam, the original Ponzi scheme. "Even if they never got anything for it, it was cheap at that price. Without malice aforethought I had given them the best show that was ever staged in their territory since the landing of the Pilgrims! It was easily worth 15 million bucks to watch me put the thing over."

At the height of his powers in the 1920s, con man George Parker was selling the Brooklyn Bridge to unsuspecting buyers twice a week.

Future business

To be successful in business, you need to be able to see into the future, unlike...

▪▪▪ **Darryl Zanuck, 20th Century Fox movie mogul, 1946, on TV**
"People will soon get tired of staring at a plywood box every night."

▪▪▪ **Satoru Iwata, President of Nintendo, 2004**
"Customers do not want online games."

▪▪▪ **Alex Lewyt, Lewyt Corp vacuum company, 1950s**
"Nuclear-powered vacuum cleaners will probably be a reality within ten years."

▪▪▪ **Arthur Summerfield, U.S. Postmaster General, 1959**
"We stand on the threshold of rocket mail."

▪▪▪ **Dick Rowe, Decca Records, 1962, rejecting The Beatles**
"Groups with guitars are on their way out, Mr. Epstein."

▪▪▪ **William Orton, President of the Western Union Telegraph Company, 1876, rejecting the telephone**
"Mr. Bell, after careful consideration of your invention, while it is a very interesting novelty, we have come to the conclusion that it has no commercial possibilities. What use could this company make of an electrical toy?"

Lottery winners who lost it all

••• **Jack Whittaker won a record $314.9-million Powerball jackpot in 2002** *but his life since then has been a chain of tragedies, arrests, lawsuits and broken relationships. In 2004, his then wife said she wished she had torn up the ticket.*

••• **In 1997, Home Depot stocker Billie Bob Harrell Jr. won a $31-million Texas jackpot** *To the former preacher, it seemed a gift from heaven until he found himself losing and loaning money at an alarming rate. As things spiraled out of control, he divorced his wife and less than two years after his big win, he committed suicide by shooting himself through the chest with a shotgun.*

••• **Janite Lee, a 52-year-old St. Louis wig shop owner, won $18 million in 1993** *but was declared bankrupt eight years later. The money was spent on generous donations to Washington University and the Democratic Party (which earned her dinner with Bill Clinton and Al Gore), houses, cars and, crucially, a gambling habit that once saw her squander $347,000 in a single year.*

••• **In 1988, "Bud" Post scooped $16.2 million in the Pennsylvania state lottery** *A former girlfriend successfully sued him for a share of the winnings, his brother hired a hit man to try to kill him so that he could inherit the cash, and other relatives persuaded him to invest in their ill-fated businesses. Within a year, Post was $1 million in debt and bankrupt.*

▪▪▪ **Callie Rogers was 16 when she won $3 million on the U.K. lottery in 2003** *She spent her money on new homes for her family, gifts, vacations, cars, clothes and breast enhancements, but was recently reduced to working as a maid to support herself and her two children.*

▪▪▪ **Denise Rossi won $1.3 million in the California lottery in 1996** *but kept the news from her husband Thomas and filed for divorce just 11 days later. When he eventually found out, he took her to court for not disclosing the money in the divorce papers, and the judge awarded him every penny.*

The woman who lost a billion When Patricia Kluge divorced her husband, American media billionaire John Kluge, in 1990, the settlement was said to be more than one billion dollars, earning her the tag of "the world's wealthiest divorcee." With interest alone on her nest-egg earning her around $1.6 million a week at the time, she felt sufficiently secure to splash out on real estate, priceless antiques and sparkling jewels. However, she wanted to create a legacy and decided that her home state of Virginia ought to have a world-famous wine region. Surprisingly for someone with such resources, she needed a bank loan. According to reports, she spent at least $44 million on the winery, a sizeable amount of which was borrowed from a bank. She borrowed another $8.5 million to develop a plot of land around the vineyard into high-end housing, and the $100 million mansion in which she lived was also financed. It turned out to be like pouring money—or in this case, expensive wine—down the drain. For although Chelsea Clinton sang the praises of Mrs. Kluge's sparkling rosé, her vintage Virginia wines did not appeal to everyone's taste. There was a distinct bouquet of panic, exacerbated when the U.S. housing crash decimated the value of her real estate. Her debts were starting to spiral out of control. By 2011, the jewels, artwork and furnishings had all been auctioned off, the mansion had been sold, and the banks had foreclosed on the vineyard, which was then snapped up by another billionaire—Donald Trump.

The schoolchildren arms dealers School lunchtime clubs usually cover subjects like stamp collecting or Mandarin for beginners, but in 2006 a school in Oxfordshire, England, set up its own arms club. Thirty teenagers from Lord Williams's Upper School in Thame formed Williams Defence to expose the ineffectiveness of international arms legislation and, under the watchful eye of a teacher, they successfully—and completely legally—brokered deals for weapons and instruments of torture from all over the world. Using the Internet, they were able to obtain quotes for a tank from Romania ($3.75 million, one careful owner), thumbcuffs from Taiwan (a bargain at $3.65 a pair) and a sting stick with barbs and spikes along its shaft for $7.50. Through an Irish offshoot—set up because brokering small arms requires a license in Britain—they also arranged deals for the sale of Pakistani grenade launchers to Syria, Turkish guns to Mali and South African rifles to Israel before winding up their business dealings and presenting their findings to the British Government.

The Nazis ran the biggest counterfeiting scam ever, and were helped by a Jewish concentration camp prisoner During World War II, the Nazis devised a scheme to destabilize the British economy by flooding the country with forged £5, £10, £20 and £50 notes. Operation Bernhard—as it was called—was the biggest counterfeiting operation in history, printing more than eight million banknotes with a total value of around £130 million ($200 million), each one virtually impossible to distinguish from the genuine article. The printing presses were based in concentration camps, where one of the most skilled counterfeiters was a Russian Jew, Salomon Smolianoff. The 140-man team was just about to turn its attention to the U.S. currency when the war ended. Although most of the notes ended up at the bottom of an Austrian lake, after the region was liberated by the Allies, sufficient numbers reached Britain to force the Bank of England to withdraw all notes larger than £5 from circulation.

The Forbidden Gardens of China, re-created in a millionaire's Texas garden Created by reclusive Hong Kong millionaire Ira Poon in 1996 at a cost of $40 million, the Forbidden Gardens outdoor museum near Houston, Texas, featured a handcrafted re-creation of the famous Terracotta Army of Chinese Emperor Qin. Although most of the 6,000 clay soldiers were in 1:3 scale, they still occupied an area the size of a football field. Then, in February 2011, it was announced that the Forbidden Gardens would close to make way for a new freeway. The terracotta soldiers were offered on Craigslist for $100 each.

Undesirable jobs

••• **Whale feces researcher** Scoops up whale dung, then digs through it for clues (21st century).

••• **Piss-prophet** Diagnosed diseases by inspection of urine (18th century).

••• **Mudlark** Scavenged in the fetid mud of London's River Thames for items of value (18th century).

••• **Plague burier** Collected corpses from homes and carried them to the nearest burial pit. The chances of catching the deadly disease were extremely high (17th century).

••• **Fuller** Walked up and down all day in huge vats of pungent, stale urine to draw grease from wool (medieval).

••• **Toad eater** Ate supposedly poisonous toads so that his boss, a quack medicine man, could miraculously cure him. The term was later shortened to "toady" to describe anyone who sucks up to his boss (medieval).

The Hemline Index Back in the 1920s, economist George Taylor conceived the Hemline Index, noting that skirts got progressively longer as the economy slowed down. In the wake of the 1929 Wall Street Crash, hems dropped almost overnight, whereas the miniskirt enjoyed its heyday in the economic boom of the 1960s.

Frederick W. Smith started FedEx after taking his last savings to Vegas In 1971, Frederick W. Smith founded delivery company Federal Express, but two years later the company was on the verge of bankruptcy with just $5,000 to its name. With insufficient money to fuel its planes and no company willing to invest, one weekend a desperate Smith took the remaining company funds, flew to Las Vegas, played blackjack and by Monday morning FedEx had $32,000 in its bank account, enough to allow it to continue operating. Today, FedEx is said to be worth up to $35 billion.

Woman lives without any money For over 15 years a woman in Germany has lived without money. In 1996, university-educated Heidemarie Schwermer gave away all her belongings and opted for an alternative lifestyle on the cheap. She travels from town to town living in spare rooms, and earns her keep wherever she goes by taking on menial jobs. She barters for food, uses self-healing techniques to cope with illness, and donates to charity any money that people give her. What's more, she says she has never been happier.

Worst trades of all time

These disastrous trades lost a total of nearly $18 billion.

■■■ *Jérôme Kerviel, a trader at French bank Société Générale, was convicted in 2008 on charges including forgery, unauthorized computer use and breach of trust after his risky trades lost the bank around* **$6.5 billion**. *Initially, Kerviel was up by more than a billion dollars, but after his trial he was fined about the same as he lost the bank.*

■■■ *In 1998, John Meriweather's hedge fund Long-Term Capital Management lost* **$4.8 billion** *in just four months after the Russian government defaulted on its government bonds. The fund's collapse triggered global panic and necessitated what was then an unprecedented bail-out by the Federal Reserve and 14 U.S. banks.*

■■■ *Yasuo Hamanaka, a copper trader with Japan's Sumitomo Corporation, lost around* **$2.6 billion** *in 1996 after attempting—and failing—to corner the copper market. He was given eight years in prison.*

■■■ *The 1995 collapse of Britain's oldest merchant bank, Barings, resulted from rogue trader Nick Leeson secretly running up debts of* **$1.4 billion** *as a result of unsuccessful gambling on the Japanese stock market. He ended up spending nearly four years in jail.*

▪▪▪ *In December 1994, the prosperous Orange County district of California declared bankruptcy after county treasurer Robert Citron conducted a high-risk investment strategy, the success of which was based on interest rates remaining low. When interest rates unexpectedly rose,* **$1.7 billion** *was lost, triggering the largest financial failure of a local government in U.S. history.*

▪▪▪ *John Rusnak, a currency trader at Maryland-based bank Allfirst, was sentenced to seven and a half years in prison in 2003 for bank fraud after losing his employers* **$691 million**. *As a result, Allfirst was sold and over 1,000 bank workers lost their jobs.*

The United States has $1.2 billion that nobody wants

A failed attempt to persuade the American public to adopt dollar coins instead of bills has created a stockpile of over $1 billion in unwanted coins languishing in Federal Reserve Bank vaults. The dollar coin-producing program has been running since 2007 and is due to continue until 2016, by which time the pile is expected to be twice as large. The cost of manufacturing these idle coins already tops $300 million.

You know when you find a receipt left in an ATM and you just have to look and see if they have more money than you? Somebody in East Hampton, New York, found one with a $100,000,000 balance.

The man who sold the Eiffel Tower—twice With at least 24 aliases, a fluency in five languages, and nearly 50 arrests in the U.S. alone, Czech-born "Count" Victor Lustig was an aristocrat among con men. He had already pulled off lucrative scams in Missouri and Montreal when, sitting in a Paris café in 1925, he hatched his most audacious scheme. Reading a small newspaper article reporting that the Eiffel Tower was in such disrepair that the French government was exploring the possibility of having it demolished and rebuilt, Lustig saw an opportunity to exploit the situation. Posing as a government minister, he wrote to six scrap-metal dealers informing them that because  the tower was too expensive to repair, it was to be pulled down and sold for scrap. The six dealers were invited to submit tenders for the 7,000 tons of metal while at the same time being sworn to secrecy for fear that news of the Paris landmark's demise would cause public outrage. When the bids came in, Lustig chose that of gullible, provincial scrap merchant André Poisson, very much a fish out of water. Informing Poisson that his bid had been successful, Lustig received a healthy banker's draft for the contract, in return for which he handed the dealer a worthless bill of sale. By the time Poisson realized he had been conned, Lustig was spending his money in Austria. Poisson was too embarrassed to go to the police and this allowed Lustig to return to Paris shortly afterwards and sell the Eiffel Tower to a second businessman.

"Eiffel Tower sold for scrap"

- **Boo.com** *spent $188 million in just six months in an attempt to create an online fashion store, but went bankrupt when the dotcom bubble burst in May 2000.*

- **Pets.com** *Despite its high public profile with a cute sock puppet mascot, Pets.com, an online business that sold pet accessories, went bust in 2000 after just two years in business, with $300 million of investment capital vanishing along with it.*

- **Webvan.com** *Founded in 1999, San Francisco-based online grocer Webvan was worth $1.2 billion at its peak and boasted of expanding to 26 cities across the U.S. It closed in 2001, putting 2,000 people out of work.*

- **Flooz.com** *started up in 1998 as an online currency that could be used as an alternative to credit cards. A total of $35 million was raised from investors, but it went to the wall in 2001, along with its rival Beenz.com.*

- **MVP.com** *With celebrity endorsements from the likes of Wayne Gretzky and Michael Jordan, online sports goods company MVP.com employed over 150 people in 2000, but a deal with CBS went sour and it was canned after barely a year.*

- **theGlobe.com** *Social networking service theGlobe.com went public in 1998, but after spectacular early success, its share price plummeted from a high of $97 to less than 10 cents the following year.*

Dotcom disasters

Crime does pay

Rich criminals at large.

■■■ **Susumu Ishii** $1.5 billion
*Japanese gangland godfather Susumu Ishii accumulated assets
of over $1.5 billion at the height of his criminal activity, partly
through real estate scams. When he died in 1991, more than
5,000 people attended his funeral.*

■■■ **Semion Mogilevich** $1 billion
*Believed to control a vast criminal empire and to be worth in
excess of $1 billion, Semion Mogilevich is suspected of money
laundering and fraud.*

■■■ **Joaquín Guzmán Loera** $1 billion
*As well as being the country's most wanted man, Mexican drug
baron Joaquín Guzmán Loera—or "Shorty" as he is known—
has amassed an estimated personal fortune of $1 billion.*

■■■ **Dawood Ibrahim** $430 million
*The son of a police officer, Indian crime boss Dawood Ibrahim
is said to own assets of $430 million in Mumbai alone. He is
believed to be involved in money laundering, drug smuggling
and terrorism.*

■■■ **Mickey Green** $100 million
*A convicted armed robber and suspected drug dealer, Britain's
Mickey Green is said to be worth at least $100 million. His ability
to evade arrest has led to him being nicknamed "the Pimpernel."*

Peter Kürten, the Düsseldorf vampire Kürten, a German factory worker who was convicted of nine murders in 1931, set himself apart from other serial killers by drinking the blood of his victims. Shortly before being guillotined, he asked his executioner, "Tell me, after my head has been chopped off, will I still be able to hear, at least for a moment, the sound of my own blood gushing from the stump of my neck? That would be the pleasure to end all pleasures." Kürten dreamed of one day appearing in a waxwork museum—and now his actual dissected (mummified) head resides in the Ripley's Believe It or Not! museum in Wisconsin Dells.

The narco Saint Jesús Malverde is worshiped by Mexican criminals as the patron saint of narcotic drugs. According to popular legend, he was a bandit killed by the police in 1909, and a number of miracles have been attributed to him. Although the Catholic Church does not officially recognize him as a saint, every year thousands of people visit his shrine in Culiacán.

The man who sued himself For reasons unknown, in 1985, Oreste Lodi decided to sue himself at the Shasta County Superior Court, California. He served the complaint on himself, took a default judgment against himself when he failed to answer, and then appealed after his case against himself was dismissed. The appeal court noted that such an action requires a plaintiff and a defendant who really ought to be two different people. In ruling, the court said it had considered asking the appellant to pay for the frivolous appeal, but decided instead to ask each party to bear his own costs. Thus Mr. Lodi both won and lost, depending on which hat he was wearing at the time.

■ ■ ■

Slavery was not illegal in the U.K. until April 2010, after which time offenders could be charged with the offense.

■ ■ ■

The mysterious bank robbery from hell On August 28, 2003, 46-year-old pizza delivery man Brian Wells robbed a bank in Erie, Pennsylvania, while wearing a bomb collar under his shirt. Police officers surrounded him in a parking lot but the bomb exploded before they could dismantle it, killing Wells instantly. Far from being just another instance of a botched robbery, the Wells case has gone on to become one of America's most baffling crime mysteries. Moments before his death, Wells had told police 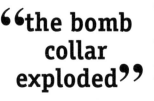 that three people had put the bomb on him and forced him to carry out the robbery against his will. So, was Wells a willing conspirator? If not, who was responsible for the collar bomb? Did he take part in the raid in the belief that the bomb was a fake, only to be tricked at the last minute?

In 2008, one Kenneth Barnes pleaded guilty to the robbery and was jailed for 45 years. He implicated Marjorie Diehl-Armstrong who, in 2010, was convicted of conspiracy to commit a bank robbery and possession of an explosive device in furtherance of a crime. She had also been found guilty of murdering her then boyfriend, James Roden, in 2003. Police say Roden could have been the getaway driver on the bank job, and that Diehl-Armstrong silenced him because she was afraid he would expose her role in the crime. Another suspect, William Rothstein, died of cancer before he could be questioned about the robbery. Although prosecutors say Wells knew Barnes and Diehl-Armstrong, the dead man's family insist he was an innocent victim. The truth may never be known.

Real dollhouse Carl Tanzler von Cosel, a German-born radiologist at the United States Marine Hospital in Key West, Florida, developed a morbid obsession for a young woman, Maria Elena Milagro de Hoyos, who was dying from tuberculosis. This obsession continued even after her death in 1931. He paid for her funeral, and, with her family's permission, commissioned the construction of an above-ground mausoleum, which he visited almost every night. Two years later he disinterred her and took her back to his house, where he kept her for seven years, fully dressed and made up. He bound her bones together with coat hangers, fitted her with glass eyes, and as the skin of the corpse decomposed, he replaced it with silk cloth soaked in wax and plaster of paris. Although investigated and charged, the case against Tanzler was eventually dropped—indeed, he was viewed by many as just an eccentric romantic!

In the 1760s, Sir John Pryce embalmed his first two wives, and kept them both in bed with him.

Animals with criminal records

- ▪▪▪ *In France in 1386, a **pig**, dressed in human clothes, was executed for killing a small child.*

- ▪▪▪ *In France in 1452, a **goat** was convicted of being the ringleader of a gang of cows that terrorized the town of Rouvre for several days, committing "much mischief."*

- ▪▪▪ *In 1471, a **cockerel** was found guilty in a Swiss court of laying an egg "in defiance of natural law." The bird was sentenced to death and burnt at the stake as "a devil in disguise."*

- ▪▪▪ *In Switzerland in 1906, a **dog** named Chomper sat in court alongside two human accomplices in a murder trial. The men were sentenced to life imprisonment and their dog was condemned to death for being a willing participant in the heinous act.*

- ▪▪▪ *In 2008, a Mexican **donkey** was thrown in jail after biting and kicking two men. It remained in custody until its owner paid the victims' medical bills.*

Chinese grave robbers sell priceless antique for 3 yuan (50¢) Stumbling across an ancient Chinese tomb, two men unearthed a number of antiques, including a painted pottery woman's figure, which they later sold for 3 yuan (50¢). Little did they know that the small statuette was 1,000 years old and worth 1 million yuan ($156,691). The pair, who admitted raiding two other tombs, sighed ruefully, "We don't know the value of things. The collector said the pottery means nothing."

Pope Formosus, exhumed and then physically put on trial, surprisingly didn't win his case Following his death in AD 896, the body of Pope Formosus was disinterred, clad in papal vestments, and seated on a throne to face a number of charges including deserting his diocese without permission and despoiling the cloisters in Rome. Singularly unable to defend himself, he was found to have been unworthy of the papacy. All his acts were annulled, the three fingers from his right hand that he had used in consecrations were hacked off, and his corpse was thrown into the Tiber.

Top tip—lost wallets are far more likely to be returned to their owners if they have a photo of a cute baby inside.

The Victorian murderess that blatantly got away with it The sordid and ultimately murderous tale of the grocer, the French girl and the vicar was the very stuff of Victorian parlor gossip—a real-life crime caper that captivated the U.K. In 1875, Edwin Bartlett, a prosperous grocer, married Adelaide Blanche de la Tremoille, a French girl ten years his junior. The marriage was soon in trouble, and within a year Adelaide had an affair with Edwin's brother. She then became friendly with a young minister, Rev. George Dyson, a liaison of which Edwin fully approved. Shortly after the Bartletts had moved to the Pimlico district of London, Edwin was suddenly taken ill and, on January 1, 1886, he died. A large quantity of chloroform was found in his stomach, but liquid chloroform burns and there were no traces of it in his mouth or throat. Adelaide and Dyson were both charged with his murder, but the case against the latter was dropped. Although Adelaide admitted using chloroform sprinkled on a handkerchief to repel her husband's sexual advances, the jury acquitted her simply because the prosecution had been unable to prove how Adelaide had committed the murder. The question of how the poison got into Edwin's stomach without burning him internally in the throat led the eminent surgeon Sir James Paget to remark, "Now that she has been acquitted for murder and cannot be tried again, she should tell us in the interest of science how she did it!" She never did.

Man's detailed tattoo places him at murder scene and lands him in jail In 2011, Southern California gang member Anthony Garcia was convicted of a murder that had remained unsolved for seven years primarily because he had an elaborate tattoo of the 2004 crime scene on his chest.

Plaintiff vs Satan In 1971, Gerald Mayo filed a lawsuit against Satan and his staff before the United States District Court in which he claimed that "Satan has on numerous occasion caused plaintiff misery, placed deliberate obstacles in his path and has caused plaintiff's downfall." The case was dismissed because Mayo had not included instructions on how the U.S. Marshal could serve process on Satan.

The strangest prison in the world At San Pedro prison in La Paz, Bolivia, inmates often live with their families and earn a living by selling cocaine to visiting tourists. They buy or rent their accommodation, and one inmate paid for a second-floor extension to be built on his cell, giving him views across the city. Writer Rusty Young bribed the guards so that he could stay at the prison for three months in order to study the activities of British inmate Thomas McFadden, who was famous for offering illegal tours of the facility. Young then wrote a best-selling book on his experiences, *Marching Powder*.

How do you like your stake? Arrested for a brutal double murder in the East End of London, England, in 1811, John Williams hanged himself in his prison cell. Not to be denied their pound of flesh, locals dragged his corpse through the streets in a cart, tossed it into a hole and buried it with a stake driven through the heart. Seventy-five years later, Williams' skeleton (complete with stake) was uncovered by a gas company. The landlord of a nearby inn retained the skull as a souvenir.

Worst torture methods

▪▪▪ **Chinese Bamboo Torture** *The victim was suspended above sharpened tips of living bamboo, which can grow up to 3 ft (90 cm) in a day. In a slow, agonizing death, the bamboo spear pierced the victim's skin and continued to grow through his abdomen.*

▪▪▪ **The Brazen Bull** *In Ancient Greece, victims were locked inside a hollow brass bull, beneath which a fire was lit. As the victim was roasted alive, his screams sounded like the bull roaring. The cremated remains were often made into bracelets and sold at market.*

▪▪▪ **The Iron Maiden** *The famous heavy metal band took their name from an upright sarcophagus with fearsome spikes on its interior. Once shut inside, the victim would either confess rapidly or bleed to death.*

▪▪▪ **The Press** *During the Salem Witch Trials of 1692, Giles Correy was placed between two large boards with weights increasingly piled on top in an attempt to get him to confess to being a witch. Shortly before being crushed to death, his last words were "more weight."*

▪▪▪ **The Choke Pear** *Popular in the Middle Ages, this device consisted of a sharpened leaflike apparatus that was inserted into an orifice in the victim's body. The torturer would then turn a screw at the top, causing the leaves to open... very slowly.*

▪▫▪ **Rat Torture** *A prisoner was chained naked on a table and heavy bowls of diseased rats were placed face down on his body. When hot charcoal was placed on top of the bowls, the rats panicked and in their rush to escape would gnaw their way through the victim's flesh.*

The Glasgow Vampire In 1954, the Hutchesontown and Gorbals areas of Glasgow, Scotland, were terrorized by a child-eating vampire. At least that is what hundreds of marauding schoolchildren believed when they were discovered scouring the Southern Necropolis graveyard after dark, armed with sticks and rocks, on the hunt for a bloodsucker. Despite efforts by the police to keep the children away, they returned every night for several days in an attempt to root out the monster. According to newspapers at the time, the horror story was so infectious that parents of hysterical schoolchildren actually asked the police if there was a man-eating vampire in the area. Authorities were quick to blame new horror comics imported from the United States. Such was the furore among adults in the local area, that the United Kingdom government went as far as banning such comics from publication, despite no direct link being found between popular titles such as *Tales from the Crypt* and the "Gorbals Vampire," as the Glasgow story became known. The elusive vampire with iron teeth was more likely to have found its origins in a local urban myth used to scare misbehaving children, but the true source of the phenomenon has been long forgotten by the children involved.

The criminal from whose skin they made shoes Wyoming doctor J.E. Osborne was so fascinated by outlaw "Big Nose" George Parrot, who was hanged in 1881, that he had his body skinned and the skin made into a pair of shoes. Dr. Osborne proudly wore them all the time, even while serving as State Governor. He also carried a medicine bag made from the skin of George's chest, while the top of George's skull was used as a doorstop by Wyoming's first woman doctor Dr. Lillian Nelson. It seems he was more useful dead than alive.

The guillotine was last used in France only 34 years ago Convicted of the torture and murder of his former girlfriend, Tunisian pimp Hamida Djandoubi was executed by guillotine in Marseille in 1977.

A killer day out—the FBI's serial killer museum The FBI's Evil Minds Research Museum in Quantico, Virginia, displays letters, greeting cards, photos and other artifacts from some of the world's most notorious serial killers. Exhibits include John Wayne Gacy's clown paintings (he dressed as a clown at Chicago children's hospitals yet murdered 33 boys), correspondence from Richard Ramirez, the "Night Stalker," sketches by Danny Rolling, the "Gainesville Ripper," and "Happy Face Killer" Keith Hunter Jesperson's handwritten manifesto explaining why he killed up to 160 people, although only eight have ever been confirmed. Before you think of taking the family, the museum is not open to the public.

A child called Brfxxccxxmnpcccclllmmnprxvclmnck-ssqlbb11116 A free-thinking Swedish couple who didn't want to burden their child with a name were fined $600 for failing to register one by his fifth birthday. In protest at the fine, they came up with this 43-character mouthful (pronounced "Albin"), which they claimed was "a pregnant, expressionistic development that we see as an artistic creation."

Colombian drug lord Pablo Escobar once burned $2 million in cash just to keep his daughter warm while on the run.

Man sues radio station after tattooing their frequency on his head When David Jonathan Winkelman heard Iowa radio station KORB offer a six-figure sum to any listeners who got its call letters and logo tattooed on their forehead, he didn't waste any time in getting it done. On learning that it was all a stunt, he promptly sued, claiming that the station was aiming to mark listeners permanently so that they could "be publicly scorned and ridiculed for their greed and lack of common good sense." To compound his misery, the station has since changed its call letters and switched from hard rock to easy listening.

The hand of glory Instead of a weapon, 16th-century burglars used to carry the pickled right hand of an executed criminal, cut off while the body was still hanging from the gallows, because it reputedly put the inhabitants of a house into a coma.

Daring prison breaks

■■■ **After six months of digging** *a secret tunnel from Saltillo Prison, Mexico, 75 convicts made their bid for freedom one day in 1976, only to find that the tunnel emerged in the nearby courtroom where many of them had been sentenced.*

■■■ **No helicopters** *or high-performance motorbikes were needed to spring Michael Mufford from the Gainesville Work Camp, Florida, in 1994. Mufford, serving time for burglary and theft, simply escaped by riding a lawn mower into the nearby woods.*

■■■ **Spotting a gang of rabbits** *raiding the vegetable patch at a jail in Uganda in 2002, five prison guards instinctively gave chase. In their absence, 31 prisoners took the opportunity to escape.*

■■■ **Trying to escape from a courthouse** *in Decatur, Georgia, in 2003, prisoner Ben N. Rogozensky fell through the roof and landed in the judge's chambers.*

■■■ **Tunneling their way out** *of a Brazilian prison in 1994, two inmates flagged down a passing car in the street outside— unaware that the driver was a prison guard.*

■■■ **Two convicts who escaped from a maximum-security jail** *in Argentina in 2010 avoided capture by disguising themselves as sheep. Wearing full sheepskins (including sheep's heads) that they had stolen from a ranch, they blended in among the local flock to pull the wool over the eyes of 300 searching police officers.*

One hundred and thirty people have confessed to the murder of former Swedish Prime Minister Olof Palme since 1986.

Next time you ring a call center, you might be talking to Indian prisoners A high-security jail in Hyderabad, India, is training inmates to learn basic data entry and keyboard skills so that they can be turned into "outsourcing providers" for local firms and, eventually perhaps, international clients.

Biggest art heist ever In the early hours of March 18, 1990, 13 paintings valued at a total of $500 million were stolen from Boston's Isabella Stewart Gardner Museum in what was the biggest art theft in history. Dressed as police officers, the gang tied up two part-time security guards and then spent over an hour removing works by Rembrandt, Vermeer, Degas and Manet, none of which were connected to alarms. *The Concert*, one of only 36 known works by Vermeer, was alone valued at more than $250 million, yet the thieves ignored another valuable painting, a Rembrandt self-portrait, despite removing it from the wall. The culprits have never been caught, and the list of suspects ranges from opportunistic local crooks to notorious Boston crime baron James "Whitey" Bulger and even IRA gunrunners. In the hope of recovering the paintings, the museum has offered a $5-million "no-questions-asked" reward while the U.S. attorney's office is offering immunity from prosecution. To date there have been no takers.

The fraudster who faked his own death by crashing his plane Faced with a succession of fraud charges that could have cost him hundreds of thousands of dollars, and with his outwardly idyllic marriage in ruins, disgraced Indiana financial advisor Marcus Schrenker decided his only escape was to fake his own death. On January 11, 2009, he took off in a light aircraft from Anderson, Indiana, stating his destination as Florida, but near Birmingham, Alabama, he made a distress call telling air traffic controllers that his windshield had imploded and that he was bleeding heavily. He then set the plane to autopilot and parachuted out at 24,000 ft (7,300 m). The plane flew 200 miles (320 km) on autopilot before eventually crashing in Florida, where investigators found the windshield intact and no sign of blood. A huge manhunt was launched by officers in three states, and after evading Alabama police by using a false name, Schrenker was arrested two days later at a campground in Quincy, Florida. He had slashed his left wrist and was barely conscious. Later that year, he pleaded guilty to charges relating to the plane crash and was jailed for four years. In 2010, he was additionally sentenced for three counts of fraud.

> "Plane crashed on autopilot"

The mobsters who used a TV show to communicate from jail In the past, resourceful prisoners have sent hit lists in the form of loving messages to family members or have stuffed notes into the pockets of visiting children while hugging them. One mafia syndicate even bought a radio station to play prearranged songs whose meaning would be understood by inmates. However, a new ploy came to light recently when it emerged that mobsters were using a TV soccer show to send coded messages to jailed crime lords. The Sunday afternoon sports program *Quelli che il Calcio* usually provides friendly banter between fans—with viewers encouraged to text in comments and jokes—but mafia hoods had hijacked it to relay secret messages regarding the shipment of drugs and other criminal activities. Their ruse came to light when guards intercepted a letter telling a jailed mobster to watch the show.

The generous fraudster For eight years starting in 2000, U.K. national newspaper journalist Lee Horton defrauded his employer out of around $600,000, but instead of spending his ill-gotten gains on himself, he donated much of it to charity, like a latter-day Robin Hood. As sports editor at *The People*, Horton invented contributors and claimed up to $600 a time for work they had supposedly done. As the amounts were relatively small, the scam was not spotted for ages, allowing Horton to spend the proceeds on his daughter's education, donating money to her school, and giving money to a Down Syndrome charity. He also paid for morale-boosting trips for his colleagues, taking them on a golf trip. When his duplicity was finally exposed, he was jailed for 15 months and forced to sell his house.

Strange deaths

- *401 BC* **Mithridates**
  Killed by scaphism, a form of torture whereby the victim was eaten alive by insects over a period of 17 days.

- *c.AD 92* **Saint Antipas**
  Roasted alive inside a hollow brass bull.

- *415* **Hypatia of Alexandria**
  Skin was ripped off with sharp seashells.

- *842* **Prince Popiel of Goplans**
  Eaten alive by rats and mice.

- *1514* **György Dózsa**
  Forced to sit on a red-hot throne and afterwards was cannibalized.

- *1667* **James Betts**
  Accidentally suffocated after being hidden in a wardrobe by his lover at Cambridge University, England.

- *1862* **Jim Creighton**
  Died from a ruptured bladder caused by swinging a baseball bat while playing for the Brooklyn Excelsiors.

••• *1923* **Frank Hayes**

Suffered a heart attack in a horse race in New York, which his horse went on to win, carrying Frank's lifeless body.

••• *1979* **Robert Williams**

First person killed by a robot at a factory at Flat Rock, Michigan.

The professional farter Once the highest-paid entertainer in 19th-century France, Joseph Pujol (1857–1945) was famous for his remarkable control of the abdominal muscles, which enabled him to fart at will. His stage name—Le Pétomane— combines the French verb *péter* (to fart) with *–mane* (maniac), making "fartomaniac." In case you've ever wondered, professional farters are also known as flatulists, farteurs or fartistes.

Pujol didn't actually pass intestinal gas as part of his stage performance. Instead, he possessed the ability to "inhale" or move air into his rectum and then control the release of that air with his anal sphincter muscles. He discovered his unusual ability as a child when, on a trip to the coast, he realized he could suck water into his anus and project it out with astonishing force. It was said of him that "he could wash your walls with just a bucket and a squat." As an adult, Pujol was known to create spouts measuring over 16 ft (5 m). He also found that by varying the force with which he expelled air anally, he could produce different musical notes and, while working as a baker, he would entertain customers by imitating musical instruments, claiming to be playing them behind the counter.

He debuted his talent on stage in Marseille in 1887, later proceeding to Paris, performing to great acclaim at the Moulin Rouge in 1892. Highlights of his show included the sound effects of cannon fire and thunderstorms, as well as playing "O Sole Mio" and "La Marseillaise" on an ocarina through a rubber tube in his anus. He could also blow out a candle from several yards away. Members of his audience, which included royalty, were known to laugh so hard that some of them passed out. With the outbreak of World War I, Pujol retired from the stage, returning to his bakery in Marseille and later opening a biscuit factory in Toulon.

The truth about Western gunslinging duels It's a standard cliché in Western movies that the gunslinger that draws first always gets shot. However, it's not just a screenwriter's ploy to heighten the drama, it's actually based on a scientific fact. Experiments have shown that that it takes 10% more time to initiate a movement than to react to that same movement, and therefore the second gunslinger always wins because he's reacting to his opponent's draw. Even so, if you're a gambling man, a safer guideline when it comes to Hollywood is to bet against the guy wearing black.

Vlad Tepes, the original Dracula The inspiration for Bram Stoker's *Dracula* was Vlad Tepes, the bloodthirsty Prince of

Wallachia (modern-day southern Romania) in the 15th century. His father, also named Vlad, was a knight in the Order of the Dragon and was therefore known as Vlad Dracul (dracul being Romanian for "dragon"). As the son of Dracul, Vlad junior was known as Dracula. Yet, he is more commonly known to historians as Vlad the Impaler because of his fondness for brutally impaling his victims on rounded—rather than sharpened—stakes so that they endured a slow, lingering death, which could last for days and provide entertainment for his dinner guests. The height of the stake indicated the rank of the victim and, horrifying as it was, impalement may have inspired the local taste for kebabs.

A German pamphlet that appeared shortly after Vlad's death described how "he impaled people and roasted them and boiled their heads in a kettle and skinned people and hacked them to pieces like cabbage. He also roasted the children of mothers who then had to eat the children themselves." In the course of his 45-year reign, it is estimated that he had between 80,000 and 500,000 men, women and children butchered. There is actually no eyewitness evidence that Vlad ever drank the blood of his victims, let alone that he was a vampire, but given his general behavior, such exaggerations hardly constitute a slur on his character.

The severed head of the 1st Duke of Suffolk was discovered in a vault in London's Holy Trinity church in 1851 perfectly preserved by the oak sawdust from the scaffold on which he had been executed 297 years earlier.

Historical misconceptions

- *Although known as the "Little General,"* **Napoleon Bonaparte was about 5 ft 6 in** *(1.67 m), which was around average height for the early 19th century.*

- **George Washington did not have wooden teeth** *A recent study of his dentures shows that they were made of gold, hippopotamus ivory, lead, and human and animal teeth (notably horse and donkey).*

- **Nero did not fiddle while Rome burned** *According to Tacitus, a historian of the time, Nero was 30 miles (48 km) away at his villa in Antium when the fire broke out in AD 64.*

- **Marie Antoinette never said, "Let them eat cake,"** *when she heard that the French peasants were starving from a shortage of bread. The phrase was reported by the famous philosopher Jean-Jacques Rousseau, when Marie-Antoinette was only ten years old.*

- *Italian dictator* **Benito Mussolini did not "make the trains run on time."** *Much of the repair work had been carried out before he came to power, and in any case the Italian rail system was subject to frequent disruptions as a result of Mussolini's clashes with labor unions.*

- **Benjamin Franklin did not discover electricity** *when his kite was struck by lightning in 1752. Electricity was already well known by this time, and Franklin was merely trying to prove* *the electrical nature of lightning. Had his kite been struck by lightning, Franklin would probably have been killed, as happened to Russian professor Georg Wilhelm Richmann when he attempted the same experiment a few months later.*

∎∎∎ **Buddha was not fat** *Siddhartha Gautama (to give him his proper name) fasted for 49 days on six grains of rice a day and was so skinny that if you poked a finger in his stomach you could touch his backbone.*

Why Valentine's Day is not romantic at all Valentine's Day may now be a celebration of love and romance, but its origins lay in the Roman feast of Lupercalia, which took place each year from February 13–15, where drunken men sacrificed a goat or a dog and then whipped women with the hides of the dead animals. Apparently, the Roman women were quite keen on this because they believed it would make them fertile. The gruesome event also included a matchmaking lottery, in which young men drew the names of women from a jar and spent the rest of the festival with them. As for St. Valentine himself, he took his name from two unfortunates called Valentine who were martyred in different years of the 3rd century AD. Their martyrdom was later recognized by the Catholic Church by the celebration of St. Valentine's Day. It is said that we can learn a lot from history, but, in this instance, a box of chocolates or a single red rose is surely more likely to reap dividends than flogging your loved one with a dead goat.

Drowning victim? Stomach pain? Nagging headache? Try a tobacco smoke enema. In the 17th and 18th centuries, European doctors relied on tobacco smoke enemas to treat a number of ailments, including stomach cramps, gout, headaches, respiratory problems, intestinal worms, "female diseases," and even to resuscitate people who had nearly drowned. They picked up the practice from the North American Indians, but it fell out of favor in the 19th century, when experiments on animals showed that nicotine—the main active agent in tobacco smoke—is poisonous.

There are only a few recorded cases of pirates making someone walk the plank Although movies and TV series depicting the golden age of piracy in the late 17th century traditionally show victims being made to walk the plank, the practice was not mentioned in print until 1837—and even then there were only a handful of instances. The barbaric Black Bart occasionally resorted to it, but most pirates either preferred to let their enemies live or, if they had to kill them, they opted for the swifter justice of a sharp cutlass.

Chinese villagers could be the descendants of a lost Roman legion There is something a bit different about the residents of Liqian, a remote village in northwest China. Many of them have Western features, such as green eyes and blonde hair, and now DNA testing has revealed that nearly two-thirds are of Caucasian origin, leading experts to suggest that they may be descendants of a lost Roman legion that settled in the area over 2,000 years ago. In 53 BC, Roman general Marcus Crassus was defeated and beheaded near modern-day Iran, and some 145 Roman soldiers are believed to have subsequently roamed the area for years. It is thought they may have traveled east, been captured by the Chinese, and founded Liqian in 36 BC.

Medieval knights were never left-handed; it was forbidden.

How to deal with a pirate—castrate and pickle him In 1741, Francisco Menendez, a pirate based in St. Augustine (modern-day Florida), was captured by the British. He was tied to a gun, and the ship's doctor was told to pretend to castrate him. If that bizarre punishment were not enough, he was later given 200 lashes and pickled (given a salt-and-vinegar bath).

The Japanese soldier who didn't surrender for 29 years after World War II In 1944, Hiroo Onoda, a 23-year-old second lieutenant in the Japanese Army, was posted to Lubang Island in the Philippines under orders to continue fighting even if his unit was wiped out. He obeyed these instructions so rigidly that he carried on fighting World War II single-handed for the next 30 years. During that time, he resisted all attempts to persuade him to surrender, convinced that stories about the war being over were merely U.S. propaganda. Leaflets signed by his chief of staff and announcing Japan's surrender were dropped on the island, but he dismissed them, along with loudspeaker attempts by friends, relatives and old comrades to talk him out of hiding. Search parties and Japanese police were greeted with a hail of bullets. He switched hideouts to avoid detection, until in 1974 he stumbled across Norio Suzuki, a Japanese student on a camping holiday. Onoda was about to shoot, but Suzuki managed to convince him that the whole of Japan was concerned for the lost soldier's welfare. Eventually, Onoda agreed to lay down his arms—but only if ordered to do so by his commanding officer. So Major Yoshimi Taniguchi temporarily left his civilian job as a bookseller to fly to Lubang where, on March 9, 1974, Lt. Hiroo Onoda finally surrendered, handing in his rifle, 500 rounds of ammunition and several live hand grenades.

❝greeted with a hail of bullets❞

Roman gladiator graveyard uncovered in the U.K. In 2010, scientists dug up 80 skeletons under the English city of York that they have identified as being from a Roman gladiator cemetery. Clues that the skeletons were those of gladiators include heads that had been hacked off, deep bites from lions, tigers or bears, and the fact that many of the dead had one arm that was bigger than the other, suggesting that the men had been trained from a young age with a weapon in one hand.

▪▪▪ **Royal escape** *In 1651, the future Charles II of England made a daring escape from soldiers scouring the countryside for him. He hid in an oak tree, and in a priest's bolt-hole in a mansion, before making his way to France dressed as a lady's maid.*

▪▪▪ **Dedicated digger** *In 1757, Italian nobleman Giacomo Casanova escaped from a lead-lined prison in Venice by digging a tunnel under his cell with a piece of iron he found in the jail yard. When he was moved to an adjacent cell, he persuaded his new neighbor to continue the tunnel and they both escaped together.*

▪▪▪ **Glide to victory** *British World War II soldiers in prison at the notorious Colditz Castle took great lengths to try and escape, going as far as constructing a two-man glider plane out of mattresses and old wood. The glider was hidden in an attic, but the castle was liberated before it could be used. A model made after the war suggested that the plane could have carried them to safety.*

▪▪▪ **Daring tunnel** *Wolfgang Fuchs of Berlin helped over 100 people to escape from East to West Berlin in the early 1960s. He dug tunnels under the wall for over 400 ft (122 m), including one that began in a bakery and allowed over 55 people to pass through.*

▪▪▪ **Skinny criminal** *In 2006, an Australian prisoner managed to squeeze out of his jail cell after losing more than 30 lb (13.6 kg). He had weighed 154 lb (70 kg) when jailed in 2003, but he had slimmed down to only 124 lb (56 kg) over three years, and was able to escape after chiseling a gap between the bars and the wall.*

Headhunters operated in Europe (Montenegro) into the 20th century.

The man who swallowed molten lead and survived On the night of December 2, 1755, the tower of the Eddystone Lighthouse, built on a rock 13 miles (21 km) southwest of Plymouth, England, caught fire. The keeper on watch, 94-year-old Henry Hall, desperately tried to put out the blaze from below, but as he was doing so, the lead roof melted and some of it ran down his throat. The lighthouse was destroyed, but against all the odds, Hall lived for another 12 days. At his postmortem, a flat, oval piece of lead weighing more than 7 oz (200 g) was found in his stomach. Dr. Spry, the physician in charge, wrote an account of the case to the Royal Society, but when the Fellows refused to believe that a man could live for 12 days in that condition, an irate Spry conducted experiments in which he poured molten lead down the throats of dogs and chickens to prove that it was possible to survive such an accident.

> **"lived another 12 days"**

The Serbian wall of skulls A tower made from human skulls stands as a monument to 19th-century Serbian rebels in the town of Niš. In 1809, the Serbs were defeated by the Turks, who ordered that the heads of the dead Serbs be mounted on a tower to serve as a warning to others. A total of 952 Serbian skulls became part of the construction, the scalps being stuffed with cotton and sent back to Constantinople (now Istanbul) as proof of victory. When Serbia was liberated, the chapel was kept as a monument, and 58 skulls remain.

▪ ▪ ▪

Chinese armies used armor made from paper In 11th-century China, the Song Dynasty began to issue thousands of suits of armor to their troops, all made from paper. They discovered that if you layered enough paper it could prevent an arrow from penetrating surprisingly effectively. The Song Dynasty was also the first government ever to produce money printed on paper. A couple of hundred years later, the Ming Dynasty was still distributing paper armor to help troops defend against Japanese invasion—incredibly, reports suggest that the armor was bulletproof. The Ming Dynasty also equipped soldiers of this period with equally useless-sounding cotton armor.

▪ ▪ ▪

The U.S. made plans to invade Canada before World War II In the 1920s, certain American strategists were concerned that Britain's imperial reach would bring it into conflict with the U.S. So they developed War Plan Red, whereby the U.S. Army would invade Canada at various locations to prevent the U.K. using Canadian soil for an attack on Washington. The plan was apparently approved by the U.S. Secretary of War in 1930 and updated in 1934, but was officially scrapped in 1939 following the outbreak of World War II.

Infamous last words

> **"**Don't worry, it isn't loaded.**"**

Terry Kath, *front man of rock band Chicago, who, while drunk, shot himself in the head, 1978*

> **"**They couldn't hit an elephant at this dist...**"**

American Civil War General John Sedgwick *surveying enemy lines at the Battle of Spotsylvania Court House, 1864*

> **"**Take a step forward lads, it'll be easier that way.**"**

Irish patriot Robert Erskine Childers *to his firing squad, Irish Civil War, 1922*

> **"**Show my head to the people, it is worth seeing.**"**

French Revolutionary Georges Danton *to his executioner, 1794*

> **"**I've never felt better.**"**

Actor Douglas Fairbanks, *1939*

> **"**Eighteen straight whiskies— I think that's a record.**"**

Welsh poet and serial drinker **Dylan Thomas**, *1953*

▪▪▪ **"***Why yes, a bulletproof vest.***"**

*U.S. murderer **James W. Rodgers**, asked if he had any final request before facing a firing squad, 1960*

▪▪▪ **"***Now, now, my good man,
this is no time for making enemies.***"**

*French philosopher **Voltaire**, when asked by a priest to renounce Satan, 1778*

▪▪▪ **"***You all brought me here to be executed,
not to make a speech.***"**

***Charlie Livingston** on death row, Texas, 1997*

▪▪▪ **"***I'd rather be fishing.***"**

*U.S. murderer **Jimmy Glass**, executed in the electric chair, 1987*

▪▪▪ **"***Tape Seinfeld for me.***"**

*U.S. actor **Harvey Korman**, 2008*

▪▪▪ **"***Go on, get out—last words are
for fools who haven't said enough.***"**

*Revolutionary **Karl Marx** to his housekeeper,
who urged him to tell her his last words so
she could write them down, 1883*

Horrible hagiography

▪▪▪ St. Anthony   **Patron Saint of Amputees and Skin Diseases**
Egypt, 3rd/4th century
Died of natural causes

▪▪▪ St. Apollonia   **Patron Saint of Toothache**
Egypt, 3rd century
Teeth broken and burned—died

▪▪▪ St. Barbara   **Patron Saint of Gravediggers**
Turkey, 3rd century
Beaten, mutilated and beheaded

▪▪▪ St. Denis   **Patron Saint of Headaches**
Italy, 3rd century
Beheaded

▪▪▪ St. Dismas   **Patron Saint of Death Row Prisoners**
Jerusalem, 1st century
Crucified

▪▪▪ St. Fiacre   **Patron Saint of Venereal Disease**
Ireland, 7th century
Died of natural causes

▪▪▪ St. Guy   **Patron Saint of Rabies**
Belgium, 10th century
Died of exhaustion

▪▪▪ St. Lucy   **Patron Saint of Sore Throats**
Sicily, 3rd century
Eyes gouged out—died

▪▪▪ St. Vitus   **Patron Saint of Oversleeping**
Sicily, 3rd century
Boiled in oil

Military hot-air balloons and submarines were used in the American Civil War The victorious Union Army pioneered the use of hydrogen gas balloons to survey the battlefield and spot enemy troops. The Union Army Balloon Corps made flights for two years under the command of famous aeronaut Thaddeus Lowe. Even more surprising is the fact that during the Civil War both sides developed hundreds of early submarines, although very few had any impact on the war. The Union made a failed attempt to launch the first U.S. Navy submarine into

"first submarine to sink an enemy ship"

battle. The *Alligator* was a hand-powered submarine, eventually lost off North Carolina in 1863 as it was being towed toward Charleston to support an attack. Thomas Selfridge, the captain of the ill-fated craft, managed to escape three other sinking vessels over the course of the war. Not to be outdone, the Confederacy developed their own submarines, the most famous being the *H.L. Hunley*, which sank twice in development, killing 12 crew and the inventor, Horace Lawson Hunley. The cursed contraption went on to make history by becoming the first submarine to sink an enemy ship, the USS *Housatonic*, before disappearing again, this time with eight crew onboard. After more than 100 years at the bottom of the Atlantic, the *Hunley* was located in 1995 and raised in 2000, when the remains of its final crew were given a proper burial.

Apocalyptic predictions...

▪▪▪ *In 1499, German mathematician and astronomer* **Johannes Stöffler** *predicted that a vast flood would swamp the world on February 20, 1524. A nobleman, Count von Iggleheim, was so convinced by the doomsday forecast that he built a three-story ark on the Rhine, and hundreds of people desperate to gain a seat on the vessel were killed in rioting, including the count. In the end, it just rained a little that day. Stöffler had more success with one of his later predictions—that his life would be endangered by a "falling body." Wisely he chose to stay indoors on the day in question, but reaching for a book, the shelf came loose and smashed him on the head.*

▪▪▪ *In 1974, scientists* **John Gribbin and Stephen Plagemann** *wrote a best-selling book,* The Jupiter Effect, *in which they announced that an alignment of the major planets on the same side of the Sun in March 1982 would spark a series of cosmic events ending in a massive earthquake along the San Andreas Fault that would obliterate Los Angeles. As the dreaded day approached, panicked Los Angeles residents bombarded the city's Griffith Observatory for information; others temporarily left town, just to be safe. A year after the non-event, the same authors published* The Jupiter Effect Reconsidered. *It, too, became a best seller.*

▪▪▪ *California prophet* **Harold Camping** *and his followers spent $100 million dollars informing anyone who would listen that the world was going to end on May 21, 2011, with a series of devastating earthquakes. When nothing happened, Camping said he had really meant October 21, 2011. In between times, he suffered a stroke. Camping had previously declared doomsdays for May 21, 1988, and September 7, 1994.*

Thomas Edison's predictions for 2011 The June 23, 1911, issue of the *Miami Metropolis* printed Thomas Edison's predictions for what life would be like in America a century later, in 2011.

"But the traveler of the future... will largely scorn such earth crawling. He will fly through the air, swifter than any swallow, at a speed of two hundred miles an hour, in colossal machines, which will enable him to breakfast in London, transact business in Paris and eat his luncheon in Cheapside.

The house of the next century will be furnished from basement to attic with steel, at a sixth of the present cost— of steel so light that it will be as easy to move

> **❝He will fly through the air, swifter than any swallow❞**

a sideboard as it is today to lift a drawing room chair. The baby of the twenty-first century will be rocked in a steel cradle; his father will sit in a steel chair at a steel dining table, and his mother's boudoir will be sumptuously equipped with steel furnishings, converted by cunning varnishes to the semblance of rosewood, or mahogany, or any other wood her ladyship fancies."

In a letter written in 1704, renowned British scientist Sir Isaac Newton predicted that the world would end in 2060.

Assassination plots to die for

••• **Embroiled in a power struggle with his mother, Agrippina, Roman Emperor Nero decided to assassinate her** *by rigging her bed so that when she lay down on it, her weight would trigger a mechanism that would cause the ceiling to collapse on top of her. Alas, he had overlooked the fact that Agrippina liked her slaves to warm her bed before she got into it, as a result of which it was a slave who was crushed to death. Undeterred, Nero tried to lure his mother onto a self-sinking boat, but when that, too, failed, he resorted to more conventional methods and sent three men to stab Agrippina to death—a case of third time lucky.*

••• **Hitler was the target of no fewer than 42 assassination attempts,** *most of which were doomed to failure from the planning stages. A German by the name of Georg Elser hatched a plan to blow up the Führer when he made his annual November 8 speech at a Munich bar, the Bürgerbraükeller. Over the course of a year, he stole explosives from a factory near his home and then every night for three months before Hitler's visit he ate dinner at the Bürgerbraükeller, hid in a cupboard until the staff had left, and then painstakingly hollowed out a pillar to accommodate his bomb. Unfortunately for Elser—and the rest of civilization—Hitler's November 1939 speech had to be cut short because of fog, and the bomb exploded 13 minutes after he had left the bar. Eight people died in the blast and 63 were injured. Elser was captured and imprisoned until April 1945 when, with Germany on the brink of defeat, Hitler took his revenge by ordering his would-be assassin's execution.*

❚❚❚ **Knowing he would only get one shot at wiping out King Louis Philippe of France,** *Corsican crook Giuseppe Marco Fieschi left nothing to chance and combined 20 guns into one lethal killing machine. On July 28, 1835, he aimed his 20-barreled contraption down a Parisian street that the king was about to cross with his sons and staff. As soon as Louis Philippe was in his various lines of fire, Fieschi exploded his machine, sending a volley of bullets in all directions except the one that mattered. Eighteen people were killed and many more (including the hapless Fieschi himself) were injured, but the king and his family emerged unscathed. Fieschi paid for his ineptitude beneath the guillotine.*

❚❚❚ **Fidel Castro has survived at least 638 attempts on his life** *since coming to power, which equates to about one a month. Many of the more ingenious schemes were instigated by the CIA, including handing the Cuban leader an exploding cigar, coating the inside of his scuba diving suit in a deadly fungus, and buying a large number of mussels, filling them with explosives, and painting them in bright colors so that they would attract Castro on one of his undersea dives. Another plot failed because a poisoned milk shake, rather than being stored in a fridge, was kept in a freezer, making it impossible to drink. A former lover was also recruited to kill Castro. The CIA gave her poison pills, which she hid in her cold cream jar,*

but the pills melted and she decided that stuffing cold cream in Castro's mouth while he slept was a bad idea. In fact, he had guessed that she was planning to kill him and actually offered her his own pistol to carry out the deed, whereupon she wailed, "I can't do it, Fidel."

■■■ **As the first emperor of unified China in the 3rd century BC, Qin Shi Huang had already survived one assassination attempt** *and had given orders for all known associates of the culprit to be hunted down. Among those was Gao Jianli, an accomplished lute player, who, after changing his name, was one day summoned to the palace to perform. However, someone recognized him and the king was informed, but unable to bring himself to kill such a skilled musician, he ordered Gao Jianli's eyes to be gouged out instead. Despite his handicap, Gao continued to play at the royal court and managed to earn the emperor's trust while secretly planning a satisfying revenge. His weapon of choice was his lute, fortified by tying a lead weight to the instrument. So it was that one day the emperor was attacked by a blind man wielding a small guitar. Gao swung the lute where he guessed the emperor's head would be but missed by some distance and was then swiftly executed.*

The bat bombs of World War II When Pennsylvania dentist and inventor Lytle S. Adams heard about the attack on Pearl Harbor in December 1941, he knew exactly how to get back at the Japanese—bat bombs. He planned to destroy entire Japanese cities by strapping tiny incendiary devices to bats, reasoning that they would penetrate every nook and cranny. Adams happened to know Eleanor Roosevelt, and so his crackpot scheme was not dismissed out of hand. Far from it, in fact, as it was taken up with some enthusiasm by the President's advisors, who wrote reassuringly, "This man is not a nut." By 1943, the U.S. Army was conducting serious tests. Thousands of bats were captured with nets, and were placed in ice cube trays and cooled so that they would be in hibernation mode when shipped overseas. However, the tests did not exactly go to plan. On one occasion, a few of the incendiary bats were released accidentally and managed to destroy a hangar and a general's car. Clearly more work was needed. The Marine Corps took over the program, but after 30 demonstrations and $2 million spent, the project was canceled as someone in high office decided that an atomic bomb might just be more effective.

The sultan with an udder fixation Ibrahim I, ruler of Turkey in the 17th century, loved big women—the bigger the better. When he noticed the private parts of a cow, he was so taken with its magnificent udder that he instructed his agents to scour the globe in search of a woman of bovine proportions. In Armenia, they found Sechir Para, who tipped the scales at a hefty 330 lb (150 kg), which so pleased Ibrahim that she was instantly made his harem favorite and appointed Governor General of Damascus.

The Texas horned lizard cries blood—and other unusual defenses This feisty lizard really pushes the envelope when it comes to warding off attackers. It forces jets of blood from its own eyes when threatened by a predator. It's possible for humans to squirt liquid from their tear ducts, but this goes one step further. It can squirt its own blood, which contains an unpleasant-tasting toxin—although regular lizard blood is not known to be particularly tasty—for more than 5 ft (1.5 m). These lizards are not alone in their disturbing defense mechanisms. South African armored crickets can not only splash blood from their insect armpits, but vomit also. The Spanish ribbed newt contorts its rib bones so that they break the skin and become a row of sharp, poison-tipped weapons. Fortunately, stabbing itself multiple times through its own torso does not seem to have an adverse effect on the Spanish newt. Meanwhile, to scare off birds, the walnut sphinx caterpillar whistles by blowing through breathing tubes in its side. Surely a candidate for *America's Got Talent?*

Oliver the human-chimp hybrid Back in the early 1970s, South African animal trainers Frank and Janet Burger bought a chimp by the name of Oliver who had recently been captured in the Congo. Yet, somehow Oliver wasn't like other chimps. He walked upright like a human with his arms swinging at his sides, he had flatter facial features than most chimps, and he liked drinking coffee and watching TV in the evening. He also preferred female human company to female chimp company. So Janet Burger decided to sell Oliver to New York lawyer Michael

Miller, who immediately sensed that his new charge was box-office gold and began promoting him as the missing link. He appeared on *The Ed Sullivan Show* and toured the world.

Miller sought to prove his claims by having scientific tests conducted on Oliver, and these reportedly revealed that Oliver had 47 chromosomes—one fewer than an ordinary chimp and one more than a human being. It appeared that he was indeed half-human, half-chimp. Then, in 1997, detailed DNA testing tore Oliver's world apart, disclosing that he had 48 chromosomes after all. He was a chimp, pure and simple. Today, Oliver, now aged over 50, lives on a reservation near San Antonio, Texas. He is almost blind, so his TV viewing days are over, and he walks on all fours like a normal chimp, but he probably still tells the other chimps about the day he so nearly qualified for the human race.

The plant of drunkenness The South American *brugmansia* plant, or Angel's Trumpet, is known locally as *el borrachero* ("the drunkenness") because it contains high levels of the drug scopolamine, which can cause disorientation, hallucinations and memory loss. In powdered form it is known as burundanga and it can be slipped into someone's drink, supposedly rendering them incapable of resistance. In Thailand, there have been reports of tourists being robbed after having their food or drink laced with burundanga, and it was recently revealed that the old Czechoslovak Communist Secret Police occasionally used scopolamine as a truth drug to obtain confessions from alleged anti-state conspirators.

The tsunami weapon During World War II, the New Zealand Army conducted top-secret experiments off the coast of Auckland to perfect a tsunami bomb. A series of underwater explosions were set off in 1944 and 1945 to trigger mini tidal waves, but the plan was never tested on a full scale. The brainchild of Professor Thomas Leech, the tsunami weapon was considered so significant that U.S. defense chiefs said if Project Seal—as it was known—had been completed before the end of the war, it could have been as effective as the atom bomb.

A bear's preparation for winter Tappen is the name given to a plug made of leaves, resin and fat that bears prepare and insert into their rectum prior to their three months' winter hibernation. They do this to stop insects from crawling in and laying eggs.

The Indian temple where rats are sacred At the Karni Mata Temple in Deshnok, India, rats are treated with such reverence that having one run across your feet, or tasting food or water that has been sampled by a rat, is deemed a blessing. The 20,000 (and rising) temple rodents are protected and regularly fed, and if anybody accidentally kills one, they are expected to buy a gold or silver rat to replace it.

In 2011, a family in Croatia sold their teenage daughter for a horse and 425 euros (about $600).

Attack of the killer cactus One day in 1982, while out in the desert in Arizona, roommates David Grundman and James Joseph Suchochi decided it would be fun to take pot shots with their guns at the saguaro cacti that grow there. First, Grundman shot a small saguaro in the trunk so many times that it fell to the ground. Sadly for him, he then became over-ambitious and took aim at a 100-year-old specimen standing some 26 ft (8 m) high. No sooner had he fired his first round than a heavy, 4-ft-long (1.2-m) spiny arm, severed by the blast, crashed down on the unsuspecting Grundman and killed him. Never underestimate a plant.

* * *

The *brontosaurus* dinosaur never existed, *Jurassic Park*'s *velociraptors* were really the size of chickens, and many dinosaurs had feathers.

* * *

Would cockroaches really be the only organisms to survive a nuclear apocalypse? The hard-to-kill cockroach is often described as the only animal that would be left after a nuclear apocalypse, but this is not strictly true. Cockroaches are about ten times more resistant to radiation than humans, but this would not protect them from nuclear fallout. However, there are many different insects that may indeed survive such an event, including a species of wasp that has been proven to withstand well over ten times as much harmful radiation as emitted by the atomic bomb dropped on Hiroshima, Japan, in 1945. However, the survival abilities of these hardy creatures pale into insignificance when compared to certain strains of bacteria found in meat, which can withstand 1,500 times more radiation than it would take to kill a human.

The islands that smell of farts The Izu Islands are a group of volcanic islands off the coast of Honshu, Japan, which, because of their volcanic composition, are constantly filled with the stench of sulfur, creating a smell like thousands of farts! The dangerously high levels of the gas forced the islands to be evacuated in 2000, and, although residents were able to return five years later, they are now required to carry gas masks with them at all times.

When Niagara Falls ran dry On the morning of March 30, 1848, people living near Niagara Falls awoke to a spooky silence. What had happened to the falls' thundering roar? On closer inspection, they saw to their horror that the Niagara River had been reduced to nothing more than a trickle. Fish lay dead and turtles floundered around helplessly while opportunists walked on the riverbed, collecting guns, bayonets and tomahawks as souvenirs. As the incredible news spread, thousands flocked from nearby cities to witness the bizarre spectacle. Mills and factories were forced to close because the waterwheels had stopped and worried souls, convinced that the end of the world was nigh, flocked to church to pray for the falls to start flowing again. Then the cause of the mystery was revealed—gale force, southwesterly winds had pushed huge chunks of ice to the extreme northeastern tip of Lake Erie, forming an ice dam that blocked the lake's outlet into the Niagara River. Finally, on the night of March 31, a distant rumble sounded from upriver, and a wall of water came rushing down the Niagara and over the falls. The ice dam had cleared. The world was up and running again.

Ham, the space chimp Three months before Alan Shepard became the first American human in space, the U.S. launched a chimpanzee astronaut. For two years, number 65, as he was known (officials were worried that bad publicity might result from the death of a named chimp) was given intensive training at Holloman Air Force Base, New Mexico. He was taught to push a lever within five seconds of seeing a flashing blue light. Failure to do so meant receiving a mild electric shock to the

"returned to Earth with a bruised nose"

soles of his feet; success was rewarded with a banana pellet. On January 31, 1961, the chimp, dressed in a mini space suit, was launched aboard a Mercury-Redstone rocket from Cape Canaveral, Florida. He performed his tasks admirably and his capsule touched down safely in the Atlantic at the end of the 16-minute flight. Only when he had safely returned to Earth with nothing worse than a bruised nose was he renamed Ham.

The space chimp's mission paved the way for Shepard's pioneering flight and Ham went on to live a comfortable existence in U.S. zoos until his death in 1983—even finding time to appear on film with another national hero, Evel Knievel.

ııı ▬▬▬▬▬▬▬▬▬▬▬▬▬▬▬▬▬▬▬▬▬

A sea urchin is basically one big eye Sea urchins don't have eyes as such, but they have light-sensitive molecules all over their bodies—in their tube feet and between their spines—so that their entire surface acts as one big eye.

ııı ▬▬▬▬▬▬▬▬▬▬▬▬▬▬▬▬▬▬▬▬▬

Egyptians didn't just mummify themselves Both cats and dogs were powerful religious symbols in Ancient Egypt, with cats representing the god of fertility, Bastet, and dogs Anubis, the god of death and funerals. Egyptians faced the death penalty if they killed a cat, even accidentally, and such deaths would be accompanied by families shaving their eyebrows as a mark of respect. Dead cat mummies would be accompanied on their journey to the afterlife by their own mummified mice to eat. All this reverence was probably not a good thing for dogs, however, as the Egyptians killed millions of them in "puppy mills," purely for embalming, before interring them in vast pet catacombs dedicated to Anubis, which are still visible today. As well as canines and kittens, mummies of baboons, cows, crocodiles, birds and foxes have all been discovered.

ııı ▬▬▬▬▬▬▬▬▬▬▬▬▬▬▬▬▬▬▬▬▬

Contrary to popular belief, bats are not blind—some have good vision and can see long distances. In fact, they can see everything but color using echolocation.

Japan's suicide forest When Seicho Matsumoto wrote his 1950s' novel *Kuroi Kaiju* (Black Sea of Trees), where two characters committed suicide in the Aokigahara Forest at the foot of Mount Fuji, he started an unfortunate trend. Since then over 500 people have taken their lives there, prompting signs to be erected in the forest bearing messages like "Life is a precious thing! Please reconsider!"

Stalin's mutant ape army Soviet dictator Josef Stalin tried to create an invincible army by crossing humans with apes. He ordered scientist Ilia Ivanov to create a mutant species that would be of "immense strength but with an underdeveloped brain." Skeletons and secret laboratories were uncovered in 2005 in the town of Suchumi, Georgia, by workmen building a playground for children. The bones are thought to have come from apes captured in the 1920s as part of Ivanov's crazy experiments, during which he seized African women and tried to impregnate them with ape sperm. When that failed, he tried to implant human sperm in female gorillas. He was finally arrested in 1930 and died in a labor camp two years later.

Radioactive rabbit poop Believe it or not, one of the legacies of the Cold War is radioactive rabbit poop. Decades ago, liquid wastes from plutonium production were dumped in underground tanks at the Hanford nuclear site in Washington State. Jackrabbits burrowed into the dumps and enjoyed the salty taste so much that they ate—and then passed—nuclear waste.

Extreme survival

76 days *adrift in the Atlantic*

Setting off from the Canary Islands for Antigua on January 29, 1982, U.S. sailor Steven Callahan took to an inflatable life raft after his sloop, Napoleon Solo, *was fatally holed at night in a collision with a whale. For 76 days he drifted 1,800 nautical miles (3,300 km) across the Atlantic Ocean, fending off shark attacks and surviving by spearing fish and drinking rainwater. When he was finally rescued off Guadeloupe, he had lost a third of his bodyweight.*

49 days *in the Amazon rain forest*

In 2007, Frenchmen Loïc Pillois and Guilhem Nayral survived for seven weeks on a diet of bird-eating spiders, frogs, centipedes and turtles. By the time they were found, Nayral had lost 56 lb (25 kg), was infested by flesh-eating parasites and temporarily paralyzed after swallowing venom from an undercooked giant spider.

11 days *at the bottom of a ravine*

Teresa Bordais, a 62-year-old grandmother, fell to the bottom of a 60-ft (18-m) ravine in the Spanish Pyrenees in 2009 and survived 11 days by sipping rainwater and nibbling on wild herbs. She was found when a red T-shirt she had left to dry on a rock was spotted from the air by a mountain rescue team.

7 days *in frozen mountains*

7 days

While snowboarding in the Sierra Nevada mountains in 2003, former Olympic hockey player Eric LeMarque became lost on the 11,000-ft (3,353-m) Mammoth Mountain. Recalling a movie scene, he used the radio signal from his MP3 Player as a compass, but during his seven-day ordeal he faced freezing temperatures and after falling into rushing water, he nearly plunged down an 80-ft (24-m) waterfall. When rescued, he was suffering from malnutrition, exhaustion and severe frostbite that necessitated the amputation of both feet.

5 days *trapped in a canyon*

5 days

In 2003, an 800-lb (363-kg) boulder fell on Aron Ralston's arm and pinned him to the wall of a Utah canyon. After five days trapped in the canyon and with food and water running low, he realized his only hope of survival was to amputate the limb. He leveraged the boulder to make his bones snap, and then, using a dull, 2-in (5-cm) pocketknife, he hacked away the muscles and tendon, the amputation taking about an hour. Incredibly, with his one remaining arm he rappelled down a 65-ft (19-m) wall and walked out of the canyon until hikers found him.

The world's most venomous insect is an ant *Pogonomyrmex maricopa*, a species of harvester ant found in Arizona, produces a sting that can inflict pain for up to four hours in humans. Twelve of its stings can kill a 4-lb (1.8-kg) rat.

How to kill an elephant Eager to discredit rival Nikola Tesla's alternating current (AC) and therefore promote his own direct current (DC) for use in the home, Thomas Edison set about electrocuting a series of animals—cats, dogs and horses—using AC to prove how unsafe it was. His big chance came in 1903 when the Luna Park Zoo at Coney Island, New York City, decided that Topsy, an elephant that had killed three handlers in three years (including one who had tried to feed her a lighted cigarette), should be destroyed. Hanging was briefly considered before Edison suggested electrocution, a method that had been used for human executions since 1890. Before a crowd of 1,500 people, wooden sandals with copper electrodes were attached to Topsy's feet and she was fed carrots containing potassium cyanide before a 6,600-volt AC charge was sent through her body, killing her in seconds. Edison reckoned he had proved his point.

What would happen if you drifted off into space? You wouldn't die immediately. In 1965, a technician working at the Johnson Space Center in Houston survived being depressurized for 30 seconds. His last memory before blacking out was of his tongue starting to boil. In fact, you would probably survive in space for a couple of minutes, but you wouldn't remain conscious long enough to be able to rescue yourself.

North Koreans are about three inches shorter than neighboring South Koreans.

Monkey suicide bombers China's *People's Daily* reported in 2010 that the Taliban were training suicide monkey bombers and teaching them to wield AK-47 automatic rifles.

The Pig War (where the only casualty was the pig) The United States and Britain almost went to war over a pig. The animal in question was owned by Charles Griffin—an Englishman who lived on San Juan Island, located between Vancouver Island and the North American mainland. The pig had a habit of straying on to the potato patch of an American neighbor, Lyman Cutler, who, in 1859, reacted to the trespass by shooting the creature dead. Griffin immediately protested to the British government and troops from both countries moved into the area.

Nobody could determine whether the pig had been poking its snout in American or Canadian soil, for the animal had unwittingly exposed a flaw in the 1846 Oregon Treaty that had established the U.S.–Canadian border. At the western end, the treaty fixed the border along the 49th parallel of latitude to "the middle of the channel" separating Vancouver Island from the mainland, but with so many straits and islands in the region, the two sides were unable to agree precisely which channel was being referred to. The Pig War dragged on for 13 years, during which time U.S. and British troops remained stationed at opposite ends of the island. No shots were ever fired. The dispute was finally settled by arbitration in 1872, when the German Kaiser, Wilhelm I, awarded San Juan Island to the United States.

Talented parasites

Check out the ingenious methods some parasitic life-forms use to further their species' chances of survival.

■■■ **Phorid fly** *Lands on the head of an ant, laying an egg that releases a brain-eating larva. The larva eventually decapitates the ant and lives in the head for two weeks until it emerges as an adult phorid fly.*

■■■ **Male anglerfish** *The male is much smaller than the female anglerfish. It bites onto the body of a female until their skin and eventually their blood vessels fuse together. The withered male then becomes part of the female body forever, useless except for his role in fertilizing the female's eggs.*

■■■ **Fungi** *Certain fungi infect caterpillars and other insects, killing them and mummifying the body as they spread. Some even turn insects into zombies, whereby the insects crawl along and die in the best place for the fungi spores to spread into the air and infect other insects.*

■■■ **Flatworm** *The flatworm invades snails, making their eyestalks swollen and colorful to encourage birds, which then attack the snails and rip off their eyestalks. The flatworms breed in the birds' guts, and other snails then eat bird droppings infected with the parasite, allowing the cycle to continue.*

■■■ **Cymothoa exigua** *This louse clamps onto the tongue of a fish, sucking blood from the tongue until it withers and dies. The* *parasite then remains firmly attached in the fish's mouth, working just like the original tongue, dining on blood, mucus and scraps of food.*

- **Tarantula hawk wasp** *This insect hunts tarantulas and paralyzes them with a powerful sting. The spider is dragged back to its own nest, where the wasp lays an egg on its body. When the wasp larva hatches, the paralyzed spider is eaten alive.*

- **Hairworm** *They begin life as tiny creatures living in the guts of insects, which they start eating from the inside until they grow to be longer than their hosts—up to 3 ft (0.9 m) in length! The presence of the worm drives the insect to seek out water, where it drowns. The adult worm then squeezes itself out of its host and lives in the water.*

- **Parasitic barnacle** *It attaches itself to crabs, invades the egg pouch and forces the crab to look after parasite eggs. If the crab is male, the parasite sterilizes it and makes its abdomen bigger, essentially turning the male crab into a female.*

Could you stop a hurricane by flying supersonic jets around it? Arkadii Leonov, a Russian professor at Akron University, Ohio, certainly thinks so. He believes that the supersonic booms created by flying jet airplanes in and out of a hurricane in elliptical patterns would counter its natural rotation and therefore disrupt it. He has even filed a patent to that effect.

Farmer cures horse with beer When one of his prize horses, Diamond Mojo, was stricken with colic, a bowel obstruction that is normally fatal in horses, Australian riding school owner Steve Clibborn feared the worst. Then he remembered an old farmer's remedy for colic—if you give the animal something gassy, it burps and passes wind and the colic starts to clear. So he gave Diamond Mojo one of his beers, and almost immediately the horse began to perk up. Steve repeated the dose of beer medicine over the following days and, once his horse had recovered, he then had to wean Diamond Mojo off the stuff.

The memory of a goldfish is not that bad Popular belief states that a goldfish's memory lasts only three seconds, but a goldfish trainer (yes, there is such a thing) has taught his goldfish to remember color patterns and the layout of an underwater obstacle course for over a month.

Stop Press: chicken and egg puzzle solved Scientists in the U.K. have used computer technology to solve the age-old riddle of which came first, the chicken or the egg. They have decided that it was almost certainly the chicken after discovering that a chicken protein, vocledidin-17, plays a key role in eggshell formation.

Where in the world is furthest from the sea? The "Eurasian Pole of Inaccessibility" in China is the place on land that is furthest from the sea at 46°16.8N 86°40.2E—1,645 miles (2,648 km) from the coast.

Earthquake power The Japanese earthquake of March 2011 had the equivalent explosive power of 475 million tons of TNT, more than 30,000 Hiroshima atomic bombs. But what does that mean? One ton of TNT is 4 billion joules, or about 4,000 hand grenades going off at once.

By accelerating the Earth's spin, the 2011 Japanese earthquake has shortened the length of a day by about 1.8 microseconds—but you probably haven't noticed.

Bats are drinking heavyweights A constant diet of fermented fruit often gives fruit bats a blood alcohol concentration in excess of 100 mg per 100 ml of blood—a level that would render humans noticeably drunk. Yet these bats can still navigate their way in and out of caves in the dark while we can't even walk in a straight line.

The rise of the stink bug Native to the Far East, the brown marmorated stink bug, which emits a foul odor through holes in its abdomen, was only introduced to the U.S. by accident as recently as 1998—yet this agricultural pest has already spread to at least 33 states.

Schmidt's sting pain index

U.S. entomologist Justin O. Schmidt classified the stings of 78 insect species and graded them according to the type and amount of pain they inflict. Some results:

1.0 *Sweat bee*

Light, ephemeral, almost fruity. A tiny spark has singed a single hair on your arm.

1.2 *Fire ant*

Sharp, sudden, mildly alarming. Like walking across a shag carpet and reaching for the light switch.

1.8 *Bullhorn acacia ant*

A rare, piercing, elevated sort of pain. Someone has fired a staple into your cheek.

2.0 *Bald-faced hornet*

Similar to getting your hand mashed in a revolving door.

2.0 *Yellowjacket wasp*

Imagine W.C. Fields extinguishing a cigar on your tongue.

2.0 *Honey bee and European hornet*

Like a match head that flips off and burns on your skin.

3.0 *Red harvester ant*

Bold and unrelenting. Somebody is using a drill to excavate your ingrown toenail.

3.0 *Paper wasp*

Caustic and burning. Like spilling a beaker of hydrochloric acid on a paper cut.

4.0 *Tarantula hawk wasp*

Blinding, fierce, shockingly electric. A running hair drier has been dropped into your bubble bath.

4+ *Bullet ant*

Pure, intense, brilliant pain. Like fire-walking over flaming charcoal with a 3-inch rusty nail in your heel.

A fire in Pennsylvania has been burning for decades
An underground coalmine fire in Centralia, Pennsylvania, has been burning since 1962. It has resisted all attempts to put it out and now covers an area of more than 400 acres (160 ha), pumping smoke, fumes and toxic gases up through people's backyards. In the early 1980s, many homes had to be abandoned as carbon monoxide reached dangerous levels and, with the fire still burning and spreading, Centralia has become

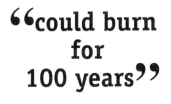

"could burn for 100 years"

a virtual ghost town. Its population was just ten in 2010, compared to over 1,000 in 1981. Although $40 million has been spent on trying to tackle the problem, an engineering study reported that the fire could burn for another 100 years.

Weird mating rituals

Male-female interaction in parts of the animal kingdom doesn't get weirder than this...

▪▪▪ *From a cast of tens of thousands of male drones, a virgin* **queen bee** *will take a mating flight with just a dozen—but the males aren't exactly the lucky few, because in the course of mating their genitals explode and snap off inside the queen, the broken penis acting as a plug to prevent other drones from fertilizing her.*

▪▪▪ *In the case of the* **mouthbrooder catfish**, *fertilization takes place in the female's mouth. She releases her ova into the water and then swallows them. When the male swims by, she mistakes the marking on his anal fin for more eggs and instinctively opens wide, only to end up with a mouthful of sperm instead.*

▪▪▪ *The male* **moth mite** *is born as a mature insect and at birth he drags his sisters out of the birth passage with his hind legs and proceeds to mate with them. He then hangs around waiting for the next batch of sisters.*

▪▪▪ *The* **male swamp antechinus**, *a mouselike marsupial from Australia, is the only mammal that dies after mating. The males devote their lives to a round of nonstop copulation and literally drop dead from starvation because they have no time to feed during mating.*

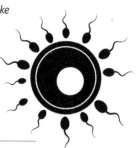

▪▪▪ *The **male tick** doesn't have a penis, so instead he pokes around in the female's vagina with his nose. When her opening is large enough, he turns round and deposits sperm from his rear on to the entrance of her orifice. He then uses his nose to push them deeper into the vagina.*

▪▪▪ *The female **praying mantis** famously eats her partner after mating—and sometimes she doesn't even wait until copulation has finished before turning him into her next meal. Yet his drive to mate is so powerful that he carries on mating even while being eaten.*

Do elephants really have their own graveyards? It is true that elephant skeletons are often found together. The idea that dying elephants instinctively make journeys to communal elephant graveyards fits with our image of the creatures as wiser than the average animal. However, the answer might be found in their mouths. Elephant teeth wear down from front to back. When the last tooth erodes, old elephants seek softer vegetation to chew, which is usually found in swampland. As these elephants are struggling to eat properly and are otherwise unhealthy, they often die in similar places. Nevertheless, elephants have been observed to move the bones of dead elephants, and appear to mourn a fallen animal, sometimes for days—even those not in their immediate families. They have even been known to bury injured or dead humans. There are a number of reports from wildlife experts and local Africans of elephants burying sleeping people under leaves and twigs overnight, thinking that they are dead!

Sharks are becoming even more dangerous to humans
By hosting drug-resistant bacteria, sharks not only pose risks to humans through their predatory nature, they may also be damaging the food we eat. Our habit of throwing away antibiotics after use has spawned a breed of drug-resistant, monster bacteria that have been breeding in the sea. These bacteria may cause virulent illnesses in sharks and fish, and have already been found in seven species of shark, including bull sharks and nurse sharks. Although we rarely eat shark, they do eat the same foods as us—other fish, crabs and shrimps—and so there is a fear that these resistant bacteria might find their way back into the human food chain.

Elephants are not afraid of mice, but they are afraid of bees While it's a myth that elephants are scared of mice, they're extremely wary of bees. New research shows that even though elephants will stand fearlessly in the face of lions, they will run for cover at the first hint of buzzing bees. Putting this information to good use, African farmers are hoping that strategically placed hives or recordings of bees will keep elephants at bay.

The jellyfish that lives forever While humans still yearn for immortality, a humble jellyfish (*Turritopsis nutricula*), measuring no more than 0.2 in (5 mm) long, has actually managed it. Like most jellyfish, it has two distinct stages in its life cycle—the polyp or immature stage, when it's just a small stalk with feeding tentacles, and the medusa or mature stage. Whereas a jellyfish of that size would normally live only a matter of hours, its secret of longevity is a process called transdifferentiation, in which it switches back from the mature to the immature stage in the nick of time and so cheats death. In effect, it constantly reverts back to its youth.

Killer whales have never killed anybody in the wild, but they almost became Marines Between 1968 and 1971, two male killer whales (Ahab and Ishmael) captured off the coast of Washington State and kept in a pen in Hawaii were trained by the U.S. Navy to attain "open ocean reliability," where they would accompany a vessel out to sea on average five times a week. The project fell into disarray in February 1971 when Ishmael went AWOL after failing to respond to his underwater recall signal. Ahab did not take part in any tests after June of that year and died in 1974.

Can trees be bad for the environment? Recent research suggests that certain trees can absorb, rather than reflect, the Sun's heat, potentially warming the Earth, and that plants, like other living things, actively produce the greenhouse gas methane. New studies also show that as climate change stimulates growth in tropical forests, the resulting increase in fallen leaves, bark and twigs could lead to stored soil carbon being released into the atmosphere.

Luckiest pig in China is saved from the pot Before the devastating earthquake that struck Sichuan, China, in May 2008, Zhu the pig was destined for the stir-fry pan. However, the earthquake saved his bacon by turning him into a national symbol of good luck. For he was buried under the rubble of his sty for 36 days before being pulled free, having survived by drinking rainwater and eating charcoal. Sparing the pig from the pot, the Chinese instead made him an honorary citizen.

What boils faster, an egg at sea level or an egg on Mount Everest? It's not a trick question; the egg takes 3–4 minutes at sea level and over 20 minutes at the height of Mount Everest. The low air pressure—about a third of the pressure at ground level—decreases the boiling point of the water, so it cannot reach the 100°C/212°F boiling point, hence the egg takes a lot longer to cook.

The centuries-old tsunami warning that saved a Japanese village in the 2011 earthquake Where modern sea walls failed to protect Japanese coastal towns from the force of the 2011 tsunami, a single stone tablet dating back more than 600 years saved the residents of the small village of Aneyoshi. The slab reads: "High dwellings are the peace and harmony of our descendants. Remember the calamity of the great tsunamis. Do not build any homes below this point." The dozen or so residents heeded the warning, and built their homes at an altitude that kept them safe from the tsunami's clutches.

A man-eating shark caught in 18th-century London On December 1, 1787, fishermen on the River Thames near Poplar landed a sickly shark whose stomach contained a silver watch, a metal chain and several pieces of gold lace. The watch bore the inscription "Henry Watson, London, No. 1369," and when contacted, Watson, a Shoreditch watchmaker, recalled selling the timepiece two years earlier to a Mr. Ephraim Thompson as a present for his son who was about to set off on his first voyage. It transpired that during a sudden storm off the coast of Cornwall, young Thompson had been thrown overboard, never to be seen again. The shark had obviously eaten him, and while able to digest his body parts, it had not been able to pass the watch and lace, resulting in its sickness, capture and death.

Rain of fish Every year in the Honduran town of Yoro it rains fish—and has been doing so since the 19th century. In May or June during a heavy rainstorm, hundreds of small silver fish are found flapping around on the town's streets, having seemingly fallen from the sky, in a phenomenon known as the *Lluvia de Peces* or "Rain of Fish." The fish aren't local to the area and may come from the Atlantic Ocean 125 miles (200 km) away, possibly sucked into the sky by waterspouts before being deposited on Yoro.

The man who took out his own appendix During a 1961 Antarctic expedition, 27-year-old Soviet doctor Leonid Rogozov saved his own life by performing an operation on himself to remove his dangerously inflamed appendix. Suffering from fever and a pain in his right lower belly, he quickly diagnosed appendicitis. However, he knew that no aid plane would be able to cope with the ferocious blizzards or reach such a remote spot in time to evacuate him, so, as the only doctor at the station, he set about conducting an auto-appendectomy on the night of April 30. He was assisted by an engineer and the station's meteorologist, who handed him the medical instruments and held a small mirror at his belly to help him see what he was doing. After administering a local anesthetic of novocaine solution, Rogozov made a 5-in (12-cm) incision in his lower abdomen with a scalpel. Working without gloves and guiding himself mainly by touch from a semi-reclining position, he proceeded to remove the appendix before injecting antibiotic into the abdominal cavity and closing the wound. The self-operation took 1 hour 45 minutes, and saved his life. If he had left it another day, his appendix would have burst. His stitches were taken out a week later and he made a complete recovery.

The ancient Egyptian pregnancy test that actually worked A 3,350-year-old Egyptian pregnancy test has been found to be 70% accurate. Each woman was told to urinate on barley and wheat, and if the grains sprouted she was declared pregnant—barley for a boy, wheat for a girl.

- **You don't lose 70% of heat through your head**—*it's more like 10%, and in fact any uncovered part of the body loses heat. The myth has been perpetuated by hat manufacturers.*

- **Being cold and wet does not give you a cold**—*they are caused by viruses, which happen to be more active in winter.*

- **Fingernails and hair don't continue growing after death**—*it's an optical illusion. After you die, skin dries out and shrinks, and it's this retraction of the skin around your hair and nails that makes them look longer.*

- **Sugar does not make children hyperactive**—*countless trials have been unable to detect any difference in behavior.*

- **Shaved hair does not grow back thicker**—*it just looks thicker because it grows back blunt-ended without the fine tapered ends of unshaven hair.*

- **Dust is not mostly human skin**—*it's a mixture of all the bits and pieces that float around, including ash, soil, powder, pollen and insect poop.*

The Church of Body Modification After being suspended four times for violating the school dress code, 15-year-old North Carolina high school student Ariana Iacono won the right to wear a nose stud in class by claiming that she was a member of the Church of Body Modification, a little-known religious group that encourages piercings and tattoos as a path to spiritual enlightenment.

Rumpology—the noble art of butt-reading Rumpology is a bit like palm reading, except you probably have to know the person better. Apparently, by studying the lines, crevices and folds on someone's buttocks, you can learn all about them. Jackie Stallone—mother of Sly—is the famous face of rumpology, and she claims that your left cheek tells you about your past and your right cheek predicts your future. British rumpologist Sam Amos claims to have read the butts of a number of celebrities, while another practitioner, German Uri Beck, has to do the whole thing by touch because he is blind.

The man who survived a firing squad On March 18, 1915, Wenseslao Moguel was captured while fighting in the Mexican revolution and was shot nine times by a firing squad in Mérida, Mexico. Unbelievably, he survived, even after a "coup de grâce" close-range bullet to the head. Cared for by the priest assigned to his burial, he eventually recovered from his injuries, although he was left somewhat disfigured. Robert Ripley discovered Moguel when traveling in the Yucatán. He hired the fortunate rebel to appear on his NBC radio show and in person at the Ripley's Believe It or Not! Odditoriums in the late 1930s.

Dead man walking—the real-life zombie of Haiti When a dead-eyed stranger introduced himself to Angelina Narcisse in the village marketplace at L'Estère, Haiti, in 1980, she immediately screamed in horror—and with good reason. She identified the stranger as her "dead" brother, Clairvius, who had been buried 18 years earlier. He told her he had been conscious throughout his funeral but had been unable to move or speak, even as the coffin was nailed shut. He showed her a scar that he claimed was the result of one of the coffin nails being driven through his face. After listening to his story, investigators concluded that as punishment for refusing to sell a piece of family land, Clairvius had, on the order of his brother, been given a dose of zombie powder (a concoction containing toad and pufferfish venoms) by a local sorcerer— or "bokor"—to induce a deathlike coma. After burial, his body was secretly dug up and he was fed a paste made from a hallucinogenic plant called devil's trumpet, which causes amnesia. This put him in a compliant, zombielike state and allowed him to be sent to work on a sugar plantation alongside other zombie slaves. However, the plantation owner was killed two years later, leaving Clairvius free to escape and he spent the next 16 years waiting for his brother to die so that he could return home. Many Haitians would ordinarily have dismissed the tale of Clairvius Narcisse as sheer fantasy, but at least 200 people recognized him following his reappearance.

People who died laughing

- ••• *In the 3rd century BC, Greek philosopher* **Chrysippus** *apparently died laughing after plying his donkey with wine and then watching it attempt to eat figs.*

- ••• *In 1410,* **King Martin of Aragon** *died from a combination of indigestion and uncontrollable laughter.*

- ••• *In 1660, Scottish aristocrat* **Thomas Urquhart** *is said to have died laughing after hearing that Charles II had become King of England.*

- ••• *In 1975,* **Alex Mitchell**, *a 50-year-old bricklayer from Norfolk, England, died from heart failure after laughing nonstop through an episode of the TV comedy series* The Goodies *in which a Scotsman fought an aggressive black pudding with his bagpipes. His widow later sent the Goodies a letter thanking them for making her husband's final moments so enjoyable.*

- ••• *In 1989, Danish audiologist* **Ole Bentzen** *died laughing while watching the movie* A Fish Called Wanda. *His heart was said to have been beating at up to 500 minutes before he suffered a cardiac arrest.*

- ••• *In 2003,* **Damnoen Saen-um**, *a Thai ice-cream salesman, laughed in his sleep for two minutes before he suddenly stopped breathing.*

Paramedic takes human foot home from car wreck for her dog Florida paramedic Cindy Economou took home the severed foot and part of a leg from a man who had been seriously injured in a 2008 road crash—to help train her body-recovery dog. Economou had been named the St. Lucie District's firefighter of the year for 2007.

Chinese man goes 55 years without an anus Mr. Wu, a Chinese farmer, spent 55 years with the opening to his rectum in the wrong place. He was born with imperforate anus, a condition that is usually rectified during infancy, but he couldn't afford to have the surgery done until he was middle-aged. In the absence of a meaningful anus, he had always opened his bowels via a small, forward, surgically-made hole—a basic colostomy—through which he used to squeeze stools out with his hands.

Einstein's brain is now in 240 slices Although Albert Einstein wanted to be cremated after his death, his son gave permission for his brain to be studied by experts interested in how the brains of intelligent people worked differently to those of "average" people. So, when he died in 1955, the famous scientist's brain was removed and cut into 240 pieces—yet subsequent research has been unable to come to a clear consensus on why he was so smart. Parts of his brain are now kept in different places, including Princeton University and, reportedly, with his granddaughter.

How to make a shrunken head One of the most unbelievable discoveries that renowned adventurer and creator of Ripley's Believe It or Not! Robert Ripley made on his travels were the shrunken heads of South America. The Jivaro tribes of Ecuador and Peru would take the heads of fallen enemies, remove the skin whole, and shrink it to the size of a fist.

Tsantas, as the shrunken heads were known locally, were used to banish the vengeful spirits of their previous owners, with their lips sewn shut to stop the spirits from escaping. When Western tourists began to visit the area in the 19th and 20th centuries, a demand for gruesome souvenirs fueled the practice, and it is said that people were killed to keep up the supply. Robert Ripley reported that a German scientist who attempted to find Jivaro headhunters came out of the forest as nothing more than a shrunken head with a red beard. A TV documentary team recently unearthed a Polish videotape from the early 1960s that not only seemed to prove that *tsantas* were still being made by the Jivaro tribe at that time, but also provides remarkable footage of the head-shrinking process.

The Jivaro used to take a decapitated head and make an incision in the back of the scalp so they could slice the skin, flesh and hair off the bone, making sure it remained intact. Then they would take the boneless head, sew the eyelids shut, and seal the mouth with wooden pegs. Next, they boiled the head for two hours in herbs that contained tannin to dry it out. The flesh was then scraped from the skin and the head was shrunk further with hot rocks and sand, before being gradually molded back into its original shape. Finally, the mouth was sewn shut with string and the head dried over a fire for several days.

The Manchester Mummy Hannah Beswick of Cheetwood Hall in Lancashire, England, had a morbid fear of being buried alive. On her death in 1758, she left a large sum of money to her doctor, Charles White, on condition that he regularly examined her corpse for signs of life for one year after her demise. So, he had her body embalmed and encased in a grandfather clock at the top of the stairs. Right up until his death in 1813, Dr. White visited the body twice a year, accompanied by a friend as a witness, and thereafter Hannah's remains were transferred to the Manchester Museum of Natural History. Finally, 110 years after her death, the trustees decided that she was "irrevocably and unmistakably dead" and she was given a formal burial.

Rapunzel Syndrome—named after the long-haired girl in the fairy tale by the Brothers Grimm—is an intestinal condition that results from eating your own hair.

The dance moves scientifically proven to help you attract women Using computerized 3-D avatars, scientists from Northumbria University, England, have conducted exhaustive tests to discover which dance moves make men attractive to women. They found that women respond most favorably to expansive movements of the neck and upper body, but not to twitchy and repetitive "Dad dancing"—the type that involves lots of arm waving that makes you look like an octopus on spin cycle.

The men's haircut that costs the same as a car The Sultan of Brunei, one of the richest men in the world, regularly pays more than $23,000 for a haircut. He pays to fly his favorite barber, Ken Modestou, first-class, from London's Dorchester Hotel to Brunei, and for him to stay in a hotel. Modestou normally charges $45 for a trim.

In moments of extreme fear or stress (such as facing execution), people have literally sweated blood, a condition called hematohidrosis, which is caused by the rupturing of the capillary blood vessels that feed the sweat glands.

The poop transplant A 61-year-old woman dying from a bowel infection had her life saved by a fecal transplant. Her gut riddled with the bad bacterium *C. difficile*, she had lost 59 lb (27 kg) in weight, she was confined to a wheelchair and had to wear a diaper because she had diarrhea every 15 minutes. So her gastroenterologist at the University of Minnesota decided to conduct a poop transplant. Using a colonoscope, he collected 0.9 oz (25 g) of feces from the patient's husband, mixed them with water and squirted them into her colon. Her diarrhea stopped the next day and she went on to make a complete recovery.

❝life saved by fecal transplant❞

Bound skulls *In parts of Africa and South America (mainly Peru), young children's malleable skulls are bound tightly so that the shape of their head is permanently altered. It is carried out either by binding the skull with rope or cloth or by strapping it against wooden boards.*

Gloves filled with bullet ants *To become men in Brazil's Satere Mawé tribe, boys as young as 12 must wear ceremonial gloves for up to 20 minutes that have been filled with bullet ants, whose sting is 30 times more painful than that of a common wasp.*

Tooth filing *Many cultures across the world practice tooth filing, the front incisors being sharpened to resemble sharks' teeth. It used to be carried out for spiritual reasons, but today it is usually just cosmetic.*

Stomach cleansing *A coming-of-age ceremony among the Matausa tribesmen of Papua New Guinea involves cleaning the stomachs of young boys to remove the female blood they received from their mothers during childbirth. This is done by pushing canes down their throats—sometimes with fatal consequences.*

Crocodile scarring *Young members of the Sepik River tribe in Papua New Guinea undergo a bloody ritual known as "crocodile scarring," where they are cut all over with razors to give their bodies the appearance of crocodile skin.*

Extreme tribal body practices

Baby born with a foot in his brain When doctors in Colorado removed a tumor from the brain of newborn Sam Esquibel, they were stunned to find a perfectly formed tiny foot and other body parts, including a partially formed hand and thigh. None had ever seen—or even heard of—anything quite like it before. They believe the parts are from his unborn twin and that the case is a bizarre example of a rare condition called "fetus in fetu'" where a twin begins to form within its sibling.

The appendix isn't completely useless—it acts as a "safe house" for beneficial bacteria living in the human gut—but male nipples and wisdom teeth are!

The strange career of outlaw Elmer McCurdy's corpse Inept at robbing trains, Oklahoma outlaw Elmer McCurdy made more in death than he ever did while he was alive. He was killed in a 1911 gunfight, his last words being the familiar, "You'll never take me alive," but it was then that his corpse took on a life of its own. When nobody came forward to claim it, the undertaker had it embalmed with a preservative and exhibited it as "The Bandit Who Wouldn't Give Up," with customers inserting a nickel in McCurdy's mouth. The attraction proved so profitable that numerous carnival operators put in bids for the mummified outlaw, but the undertaker resisted all offers until being duped by a man claiming to be McCurdy's long-lost brother. Led to believe that McCurdy was to be given a proper burial, the undertaker handed him over, only to see him exhibited by a traveling carnival two weeks later. For the next 60 years, McCurdy's body was sold to various wax museums and carnivals, although one haunted house proprietor in South Dakota turned it down because he did not think it was sufficiently lifelike.

Then, in 1976, during the filming of an episode of the TV series *The Six Million Dollar Man* at the California amusement park The Pike, a crew member moving what he thought was a mannequin hanging from a gallows got the shock of his life when the arm fell off to reveal mummified human remains. It was Elmer McCurdy. The following year he was finally buried in Oklahoma, the state medical examiner ordering that his casket be buried in concrete so that his corpse would never be disturbed again.

King Harold II of England had a number of tattoos, which were used to identify his body after he was killed at the Battle of Hastings in 1066.

There is an illness that makes some people get drunk without touching a drop Some people with Dysfunctional Gut Syndrome have been found to have blood alcohol levels above the legal drinking and driving limit—even though they haven't had an alcoholic drink. Patients with severe DGS are often put on antibiotics, which can encourage yeast growth. If they also eat a lot of carbohydrates, the resulting fermentation can render them officially drunk. It's called Auto-Brewery Syndrome.

Prolific fathers

Think your one, two or three kids are driving you nuts? Spare a thought for these guys...

■■■ 889 children

Moulay Ismaïl Ibn Sharif, Moroccan Emperor in the 17th century, produced 889 children from a harem of more than 500 women.

■■■ 360 children

Augustus II The Strong, King of Poland, 17th century, sired just one heir, but an estimated 360 illegitimate children.

■■■ 210 children

Sobhuza II, King of Swaziland in the 20th century, had a grand total of 210 children from 70 wives, plus 1,000 grandchildren, at his death in 1982.

■■■ 94 children

Ziona Chana, an Indian religious leader alive today, has 94 children and 39 wives all living together in the same 100-room mansion.

■■■ 81 children

King Mongkut of Siam, Thailand (the "King" in *The King and I*), in the 19th century, fathered 81 children from 27 mothers.

When you are angry, you can hear more through your right ear, so an apology is more likely to be accepted if it is delivered into the right ear, rather than the left.

The Russian company that will freeze your brain forever

Russian cryonics company KrioRus is promising clients life after death by freezing their brains and/or bodies until technology has advanced sufficiently to bring them back to life. It charges $10,000 for a brain freeze and $30,000 for a full body—payable upfront—and already has four human bodies and eight people's heads stored in liquid nitrogen-filled metal vats. Before you get too excited, cryonics is illegal in most countries and there's no money-back guarantee.

Sufferers of Olfactory Reference Syndrome believe that they smell bad when actually they don't.

Want to lose weight? Try a jar of sanitized tapeworms

Yes, you can lose weight on the tapeworm diet, which was actually promoted in the late 19th century. Simply ingest a nice, clean tapeworm and it will eat all the food you eat, thereby absorbing your body's nutrients and calories and helping the pounds fall off. However, it will leave you with a gross pot belly, which probably isn't what you had in mind when starting out on your weight-loss regime, and when you have reached your ideal weight you will need to flush out the

6-ft-long (1.8-m) monster that is living inside you along with its millions of offspring. Oh, and another thing: the tapeworm's reproductive system will leave your body riddled with cysts, possibly leading to brain damage and blindness.

The incredible performer who thrust swords right through his torso for fun Dutch showman Mirin Dajo made a career out of standing bare-chested while his assistant ran him through with a series of fencing foils, the blades passing through and among his major organs. Promotional photos showed him jogging with a rapier right through his abdomen and he also claimed to have survived being shot through the head twice from a distance of two feet, showing off two scars— one in the center of his forehead, the other above his right eye. He swallowed glass and razor blades, but said he never felt any pain. According to reports of the time, doctors who studied his routine at close quarters were completely baffled and could find no evidence of fakery. Dajo boasted that he was invulnerable, and few had any reason to doubt him until he died in 1948 at age 35 from an aortic rupture, caused by swallowing a long steel needle.

Joking disease Everyone knows that Dads always tell the worst jokes, but you may have a sound medical excuse for your excruciating puns. Witzelsucht—also known as "joking disease"—is an obscure brain disorder that causes people to tell corny jokes.

Cotard Delusion (or Walking Corpse Syndrome) is a rare psychiatric disorder in which people become convinced that they are dead, or that their body is putrefying or that they have lost their blood or internal organs.

The man with two faces Chang Tzu Ping was born with a second face, consisting of a mouth, a tongue, several teeth, a patch of hair, and vestiges of eyes, ears and a nose. When Chang opened his mouth, his second mouth opened too. In the small Chinese village where he lived, he was called "Two-Faced Chang" and was feared by local children who thought he was a monster.

> **"born with a second face"**

Around the late 1970s, by which time Chang was in his forties, a group of American soldiers found him and took him back to the U.S., where his second face was surgically removed. He was then able to return to his native village as the man with one face.

The man with the golden nose Danish astronomer Tycho Brahe lost part of his nose in a duel in 1566, and, for the remaining 35 years of his life, he wore a replacement nose made of gold and silver (and probably copper), using paste as an adhesive to keep it in place. He may also have used the paste to polish his nose from time to time. Brahe is a popular wax sculpture in Ripley's Believe It or Not! museums around the world.

▪▪▪ Lazarus Colloredo and his parasitic twin brother

Lazarus (1617–?) had his parasitic twin brother Joannes permanently dangling—not fully conscious but alive—from his chest. Joannes didn't speak and always kept his eyes closed and mouth open, although if he was poked in the breast, he would move his hands, ears and lips. The conjoined twins were born in Genoa, Italy, and Lazarus soon realized he could make a living from his predicament, exhibiting himself and his brother all over Europe. When not on show, Lazarus simply covered Joannes with a cloak to hide him from view. Unlikely as it may seem, Lazarus is believed to have married and fathered several healthy children—with his brother always present but not watching.

▪▪▪ Grace McDaniels, the mule-faced woman

Grace (1888–1958) suffered from Sturge-Weber Syndrome, a congenital condition that gave her a badly distorted face that worsened with age. After winning an ugly woman contest, she joined a freak show, where her face became so misshapen that she could hardly speak. Sideshow customers were known to faint just at the sight of her.

▪▪▪ Jeanie—The Half Girl

Born without legs in Indiana, Jeanie was just 2 ft 6 in (76 cm) tall as an adult and, billed as "The Half Girl," she appeared at fairs and circuses across the U.S. At one sideshow she met her future husband, Al Tomaini, a giant whose 8-ft (2.4-m) stature added a new dimension to her act. They retired in the 1940s to live in Florida, where Jeanie died in 1999, aged 82.

▪▪▪ Francesco Lentini, the three-legged man

Born in Rosolini, Italy, Francesco (1889–1966) had his malformed twin brother's leg attached to his side, and a small footlike growth on his third leg, technically giving him four feet, each of different lengths, and 16 toes. Arriving in the U.S. at the age of eight, he became an overnight sensation and went on to appear in sideshows for more than 40 years, delighting audiences by kicking a ball with his extra leg and sitting on it as if it were a bar stool.

▪▪▪ Lionel, the lion-faced man

Stephan Bibrowski (1891–1932) suffered from hypertrichosis or "werewolf disease," which left his face and body covered in 8-in-long (20-cm) hair, giving him the appearance of a lion. His Polish mother claimed the condition was caused by the fact that when she was pregnant with Stephan she saw her husband being mauled by a lion. She considered the boy to be an abomination and, at age four, she handed him over to a German impresario who gave him his stage name and started exhibiting him across Europe. Stephan later made his name in the U.S. with the Barnum & Bailey Circus, belying his fearsome looks by being elegantly dressed and speaking five languages.

Russell Parsons of Hurricane, West Virginia, has his funeral and cremation instructions tattooed on his arm. His recipe for cremation reads "Cook @1700-1800 for 2 to 3 hours."

Sticking your tongue out when you are trying to concentrate does actually increase your brainpower The natural movement of your tongue usually uses a lot of your brain's attention. So sticking your tongue out reduces that movement and leaves your brain free to focus on what you are trying to do.

The blue people of Kentucky In the early 1980s, doctors in Kentucky were understandably alarmed when Benjy Stacy was born dark blue in color. Tests revealed nothing untoward until the baby's grandmother said, "Have you ever heard of the blue Fugates of Troublesome Creek? My grandmother Luna on my Dad's side was a blue Fugate. It was real bad in her."

Martin Fugate had moved to Kentucky in 1820. He had a condition called methemoglobinemia, a rare hereditary blood disorder that gave his skin a blue hue, like a cartoon character Smurf. Methemoglobinemia is a recessive gene, which means it can only be passed on if both parents carry the gene. As chance would have it, Martin Fugate's wife, Elizabeth Smith, also had the gene and of their seven children, four were blue. Unfortunately, the Fugates didn't get out much and kept marrying first cousins or near neighbors (including the Smiths), so that soon blue people abounded in the remote hills of Kentucky. Benjy Stacy's parents were ninth generation Fugates. Happily, by the 1980s, medicine had advanced sufficiently for a cure to be at hand. Benjy and the other Fugates were injected with a dark blue dye called methylene blue, and within minutes their skin had lost its distinctive tinge—a happy ending to 160 years of feeling blue.

The millionaire body snatcher—and how much is your body worth? In 2008, U.S. dentist-turned-body snatcher Michael Mastromarino was sentenced to 18–54 years in prison for stealing from the dead and selling body parts for medical research and transplants. Among his victims was veteran broadcaster Alistair Cooke, whose bones were sold for $11,000. Mastromarino made millions of dollars by removing parts from the corpses of at least 1,000 people. Here's how much your body is worth in the marketplace today (assuming you have looked after it reasonably well)...

- **Heart valves** *$7,000 each*, and since we each have four, that makes *a potential $28,000*

- **Corneas** *$6,000 a pair*

- **Tendons** *$1,000 each*

- **Spine** *$900*

- **Shoulders** *$510 each*

- **Forearms and hands** *$383 each*

What is the point of hiccups? The precise point of hiccups had eluded the finest medical minds for years until, in 2003, a group of French scientists suggested that hiccups are an evolutionary leftover from the days when our ancestors lived in water. Primitive air breathers such as lungfish and frogs push water across their gills by squeezing their mouth cavity while closing the glottis (the space between the vocal cords at the back of the throat) to stop water entering the lungs. When we hiccup, we use ancient muscles to close the glottis while sucking in air, so it seems that the brain circuitry controlling gill ventilation in those early creatures has persisted into modern mammals, including humans. The next time you complain about not being able to get rid of your hiccups, spare a thought for Charles Osborne of Iowa, whose attack started in 1922 while he was trying to weigh a hog for slaughter and continued unabated for 68 years until 1990—an estimated 430 million hiccups later. No sooner was he cured than he died.

Why is Ozzy Osbourne still alive? Scientists are mapping his DNA to find out Despite decades of relentless drug and alcohol abuse, "Prince of Darkness" Ozzy Osbourne is still very much alive—and scientists in Massachusetts want to find out why. So they are mapping the heavy metal singer's entire DNA to see if that offers any clues as to his longevity, or whether, as Ozzy himself says, he is simply a "modern miracle."

What does the length of your fingers say about you? If you divide the length of your second finger (index finger) on your right hand by the length of the fourth finger (ring finger) from the crease where the finger joins the hand to the fingertip, you have what is known as a digit ratio. A longer index finger will produce a digit ratio of higher than one, while a longer ring finger will give a ratio of less than one. So what, you might say? Well, scientists believe that the 2D:4D ratio is the key to many aspects of men's health, behavior and career.

The boy who spent his life in a bubble David Vetter (1971–84) was born with severe combined immunodeficiency, a rare inherited disease, which meant that his immune system didn't work. As a result he could not be exposed to germs and had to live his life in a large, sterile plastic bubble. People could only handle him by wearing special plastic gloves attached to the wall of his bubble, and all water, food and clothes were disinfected beforehand. He had his own TV in the bubble and once went to the movies in his transport bubble (a smaller model built to take him from home to the Texas Children's Hospital) to see *Return of the Jedi*. In 1977, NASA researchers made him a special suit that would allow him to leave the bubble and walk around outside, but David was afraid of it, believing it to be full of germs, and only wore it seven times. The boy in the bubble, as he became known, sadly died at age 12 following an unsuccessful bone marrow transplant from his sister.

Alcohol saves drunk man from freezing A drunk man found lying on a frozen Polish park bench in only his underwear survived because the high level of alcohol in his blood acted like antifreeze. Alexsander Andrzej, 32, was spotted in the

Warsaw park in temperatures of –5°C (23°F) and taken to a hospital where a police breathalyzer showed he had 1,024 mg of alcohol per 100 ml—nearly 30 times the legal limit for driving. Doctors said the amount of alcohol in his blood saved him, although it could also explain how he came to end up on a frozen park bench in his underpants in the first place.

What did the heaviest man in the world have for breakfast? Walter Hudson of New York lived on an average daily diet of 2 boxes of sausages, 1 lb (453 g) of bacon, 12 eggs, 1 loaf of bread, 4 hamburgers, 4 cheeseburgers, 8 portions of fries, 3 ham steaks, and 2 chickens. In 1987, he became wedged in the doorway to his bathroom and had to be extricated by the fire department. It was estimated—the scales broke at 1,000 lb (453 kg)—that Hudson weighed an astonishing 1,400 lb, heavier than an original 1959 Mini Cooper. He measured more than 8 ft (2.4 m) around the waist.

If you suffer from Capgras Delusion you become convinced that a close family member has been replaced by an identical imposter.

No arms, no legs, but they could still ride a bike Even though Charles B. Tripp had no arms and Eli Bowen had no legs, they were able to ride a bicycle—together. Known to American circus audiences as "The Armless Wonder" and "The Legless

Wonder" respectively, they simply combined their attributes on a tandem bicycle, Tripp pedaling with his legs and Bowen steering with his arms.

Somebody bought Napoleon's penis for $3,000 in 1977 The French emperor's member was allegedly pocketed by his doctor during the autopsy and over a century later in 1927 it was exhibited in Manhattan, prompting *Time* magazine to remark that Napoleon lived up to his reputation for being "short of stature." Nevertheless, 50 years later, a U.S. urologist went to great lengths to buy it for $3,000 and his family has subsequently resisted offers of $100,000 for the prized possession.

Phineas Gage, the man who survived an iron bar blasted through his skull On September 13, 1848, Phineas Gage was foreman of a work gang blasting rock for a railroad company near Cavendish, Vermont. He had been using explosives to clear space for the tracks by packing gunpowder into holes in the rock with a heavy iron rod when a spark ignited the powder and sent the rod flying straight through his head. It entered on the side of his face, passed behind his left eye and emerged out of the top of his head, eventually landing some 80 ft (24 m) away "smeared with blood and brain." Amazingly, within minutes Gage was able to speak and walk unaided, but when a physician arrived to examine him, Gage vomited and brought up "about half a teacupful of the brain." Over the following weeks, Gage made a steady recovery from his horrific accident and was physically able for the remaining 12 years of his life, although the damage to his brain significantly altered his character to the point that friends saw him as "no longer Gage." His injury became famous in medical circles, and helped scientists understand that damage to specific regions of the brain—in this case the left frontal lobe—could affect personality and behavior.

Galileo's fingers and tooth found after more than 100 years Two fingers and a tooth belonging to 16th-century Italian astronomer Galileo Galilei resurfaced in 2009, 104 years after going missing. A collector bought them at auction and gave them to Florence's History of Science Museum in Italy. Scientists had cut the body parts—plus another finger and a vertebra—from Galileo's body in 1737, 95 years after his death, when the Catholic Church, who had previously branded him a heretic for supporting the belief that the Earth rotated around the Sun, decreed that he could be reburied in consecrated ground.

The first U.S. cremation Long considered a barbaric custom, by the mid-19th century cremation had started to acquire newfound respectability thanks to public health campaigners who said that cemeteries were breeding grounds for germs and toxins. In 1876, the New York Cremation Society had been eagerly waiting for a body to burn, and its prayers were answered with the death of a Bavarian aristocrat, Baron de Palm, who had stated that he wished to be cremated.

A crowd of 2,000 turned up to watch the initial ceremony, during which a riot nearly broke out after a Methodist preacher voiced his objections. Amid the ongoing controversy, the baron's body was embalmed and it was another six months before he was finally cremated on December 6, 1876.

Abraham Lincoln's grave robbers When Ben Boyd, a talented engraver of counterfeit U.S. currency plates, was arrested and jailed, the rest of his gang of forgers ran short of money. So, in 1876, two of their number, Terrence Mullins and Jack Hughes, hatched a plot to steal the body of Abraham Lincoln from the grave in Springfield, Illinois, where it had lain since the President's assassination 11 years earlier. The idea was to demand Boyd's release from jail, along with a $200,000 ransom, in return for Lincoln's corpse. However, a Secret

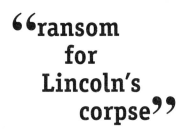

"ransom for Lincoln's corpse"

Service agent had infiltrated the gang. At the cemetery, the men sawed the lock off Lincoln's tomb and pryed the lid off the sarcophagus, but detectives swooped in before the coffin could be removed.

Since, at the time, there was no Illinois state law making grave robbing a crime, the culprits were only charged with attempted larceny and conspiracy. They were sentenced to just one year in jail—a lenient sentence for kidnapping a president, albeit a dead one.

Looking for "The Bloop" On several occasions during the summer of 1997, the U.S. National Oceanic and Atmospheric Association detected a powerful, unexplained underwater sound emanating from a remote point in the South Pacific. The low-frequency sound lasted for about a minute and was loud enough to be picked up by sensors over 3,000 miles (4,800 km) away. Investigating "The Bloop," as they called it, the NOAA eliminated the possibility that it was man-made, emitted by either a submarine or a bomb, and also ruled out undersea volcanoes or earthquakes. Instead, the Bloop's audio profile suggested that the sound was made by a living creature, even though its noise was many times louder than the loudest recorded biological sound. Cryptozoologists have speculated that it could be from a giant sea monster, something several times bigger than the largest known living creature. For now, at least, it remains a mystery of the deep.

The malignant meteorite that made a village sick On September 15, 2007, a meteorite crashed to Earth near the village of Carancas, Peru, the impact creating a large crater from which boiling water and fetid, noxious gases began to spew. Over 200 curious villagers who approached the site quickly started feeling unwell, complaining of diverse symptoms including nausea, headaches, diarrhea and vomiting. Local livestock died. Learning that the groundwater in the area contained arsenic compounds, experts initially believed that the residents had suffered arsenic poisoning caused by inhaling the vapor of the boiling arsenic-contaminated water, but further investigations revealed that the arsenic content in the groundwater was no higher than that of the local drinking water. Instead, they think the sickness may have been caused by the vaporization of troilite, a sulfur-bearing compound present within the meteorite in large quantities, and which would have melted on impact. The villagers recovered after a few days, but were probably left wishing that the Peruvian government had warned them earlier to avoid "the glowing object that fell from the sky."

Was the *Mona Lisa* a man? For centuries, art experts have debated the reason behind *Mona Lisa*'s enigmatic smile, but now it appears the secret she is hiding could be that she is really a man. According to Italian art historian Silvano Vinceti, the model for Leonardo da Vinci's masterpiece was not a woman, but one of the artist's muses, a young man called Gian Giacomo Caprotti, also known as Salai. His nose and mouth bear striking resemblances to those of *Mona Lisa*, and, using high magnification, Vinceti claims to have found the letter "S" in *Mona Lisa*'s eyes, which could be a reference to Salai. However, other experts say that any symbols in her eyes are simply cracks that have slowly developed in the oil painting over the years.

The explorer searching for $10 billion worth of treasure on Robinson Crusoe Island Located some 400 miles (645 km) west of Chile, Robinson Crusoe Island (formerly Juan Fernandez Island) is the spot where Scottish sailor Alexander Selkirk was marooned for four years and four months in 1704, a true story immortalized in Daniel Defoe's classic *Robinson Crusoe*. According to legend, Inca treasure is buried there, comprising 800 barrels of gold and jewels worth an estimated $10 billion. For over 12 years, Chicago millionaire Bernard Keiser has been trying to locate the buried treasure, but to no avail. He has already spent $2 million on the search, and, in 2010, he announced that he was shelling out another $100,000 for a fifth trawl of the island, this time using highly sophisticated mining video technology.

Pilots reveal famous Area 51 UFOs were probably top-secret aircraft It was not until 2003 that the U.S. government even acknowledged the existence of Area 51, the top-secret military base in the Nevada Desert, so it is hardly surprising that it has been at the heart of so many conspiracy theories. These include...

- *Crashed alien spacecraft are stored there and extraterrestrials are kept in freezers.*

- *Meetings have been conducted there with aliens.*

- *Plans to control the weather are being developed there.*

- *Time-travel technology is being created there.*

- *The 1969 Apollo Moon landings were faked and really took place at Area 51.*

Then in 2007, after being sworn to secrecy for nearly 50 years, Area 51 veterans were finally free to speak out about what went on there. They saw top-secret aircraft but no aliens— definitely, no aliens. They did, however, acknowledge that commercial pilots watching from below the disk-shaped fuselage of the supersonic A-12 spyplane as it sped through the sky at high altitudes could easily have mistaken it for a UFO.

What are the chances of meeting an alien? Devised by Frank Drake at the National Radio Astronomy Observatory in Green Bank, West Virginia, in 1961, the Drake Equation is the method of choice for those wishing to calculate the number of advanced civilizations in our galaxy with whom we may one day communicate. It factors in things like the number of stars in the galaxy, the number of planets around the average star and the percentage of those planets that might develop intelligent life. The latest estimates put the chances of our finding an alien life form capable of communicating with us at 0.00000003%, or, to put it another way, slim.

Is it a bird? Is it a plane? No, it's astronaut pee After several people contacted astronomy and weather websites to report seeing a glowing streak of light in the night sky above North America, NASA revealed that it was caused by a falling block of astronaut urine. The heavenly display was the result of the space shuttle *Discovery* dumping nearly two weeks' worth of astronaut waste.

The crystal skulls During the 19th and early 20th centuries, at least 13 beautiful but eerie crystal skulls—found at various locations in Central and South America—were presented to museums and collectors. Yet, despite exhaustive tests, nobody has been able to verify when and how they were made. They could be 35,000 years old, possibly carved with diamonds, but for ancient people to have hand carved a single piece of rock crystal in that way would have taken around 300 years in man-hours. Alternatively, they could have been manufactured in the 19th century with modern tools. Legend links

"prevent an apocalyptic catastrophe"

the skulls to the ancient Mayan civilization, whose calendar ends on December 21, 2012. It is said that if the 13 skulls are reunited, it will prevent an apocalyptic catastrophe from occurring on that date. So perhaps we won't have long to wait to find out the answer to the mystery.

The New York sea serpent Thousands of New Yorkers were fooled by a sea serpent constructed by German archeologist Albert Koch. He unveiled the 114-ft-long (35-m) skeleton of what he claimed was an extinct marine reptile at Broadway's Apollo Saloon in 1845. Soon, visitors paying 25 cents a head flocked to view the monster, which Koch said he had dug up on an expedition to Alabama. Then an anatomist exposed the serpent as a fraud, revealing that it was actually a composite of several specimens of an extinct whale called a zeuglodon. A typical zeuglodon measured only 40 ft (12 m) long. Koch had simply joined a few bits and pieces together.

Oak Island mystery For over 200 years, the riddle of what lies buried beneath Oak Island off the coast of Nova Scotia has been Canada's most compelling treasure mystery. A stone found back in 1803 bore a series of symbols which one expert—who just happened to be involved with a treasure-hunting company that was trying to sell stocks—deciphered to read, "Forty feet below, two million pounds are buried." Everyone took him at his word, but numerous expeditions to uncover the fabled Oak Island money pit proved unsuccessful, claiming six lives in the process. Now it appears they may all have been wasting their time because researcher Keith Ranville has come up with a new translation for the stone's series of shapes, lines and dots— and he reckons the treasure is not on Oak Island at all, but on neighboring Birch Island. Or, of course, the treasure may not exist at all.

The two Englishmen who started the crop circle phenomenon Throughout the 1980s, crop circles regularly appeared overnight in the middle of English fields, their intricate, symbolic designs leading some to speculate that they were the work of alien forces. However, with no little green men caught in the act, the origins of the circles remained a mystery. Then, in 1991, pranksters Doug Bower and Dave Chorley came forward to reveal that they had been behind the phenomenon, having created more than 200 crop circles since 1978. They explained how, inspired by an Australian crop circle account from the 1960s, they had made the circles using nothing more sophisticated than a plank of wood, a length of rope, and a baseball cap fitted with a wire loop to help them walk in a straight line. They even gave a demonstration of their art in an attempt to silence the skeptics. Yet some experts remained unconvinced, their doubts reinforced by the appearance of further crop circles, bigger and bolder in design. So, are these the work of copycat imitators or is something genuinely spooky going on in the English countryside?

Is the FBI's UFO document based on a hoax? A 1950 memo released 61 years later on the FBI website "The Vault" appears to confirm that flying saucers had been recovered in New Mexico in the years following World War II. The document states that the craft were "circular in shape with raised centers, approximately 50 feet in diameter" and that "each one was occupied by three bodies of human shape but only 3 feet tall, dressed in metallic cloth." However, research indicates that while the memo itself is genuine, the story on which it was based is almost certainly a hoax perpetrated by unscrupulous businessman Silas Newton, who wanted oil company investors to believe that he had secret alien technology that could be used to locate oil underground. The memo was probably written because the FBI and the U.S. Air Force were frequently in dialogue about reported UFO sightings at a time when the

American nation was fearful of attack by the Soviet Union as well as by men from Mars.

Mystery spy transmissions Over the past decade, a series of people have been charged with spying for Cuba against the United States by decoding messages broadcast from "numbers stations." These are shortwave radio stations that broadcast artificially generated (usually female) voices reading sequences of numbers, words and letters, which, when deciphered, allegedly relay messages to spies. Sometimes, the messages are said to take the form of tunes or Morse code. Naturally enough, no government has actually admitted to operating a numbers station, but the suspicion is there. This probably explains the interest in UVB-76, or "The Buzzer," a mysterious shortwave radio station that has been operating since 1982 and whose output consists of a monotonous buzz repeated 24 hours a day, occasionally interrupted by a Russian voice. Its purpose remains unclear, but it is safe to say that it is not drive-time entertainment.

Alien arrival A 2010 April Fool's report in a Jordanian newspaper wreaked havoc in one town. Its front-page article described a UFO landing near Jafr, 185 miles (300 km) from Amman. Residents panicked, keeping their children from school—and Jafr's mayor even sent security forces in search of the aliens. He was at the point of emptying the town of its 13,000 residents when newspaper journalists came clean.

Hacker alert

■■■ *Australian Prime Minister Julia Gillard's e-mail and the e-mails of up to ten other government ministers were said to have been hacked in February 2011.* **Thousands of potentially sensitive e-mails were hacked** *before the intrusion was stopped. Australian intelligence agencies had been tipped off about the security breach by the CIA and the FBI, although how they came to know about it was not disclosed. The Australian National Audit Office discovered that around 20% of passwords used at various Australian government agencies, including the Department of the Prime Minister and Cabinet, could be cracked in just one hour using a "brute force" approach.*

■■■ *A 14-year-old Irish schoolboy hacker who* **managed to break into the online servers for** *Call of Duty: Modern Warfare 2 and start a phishing scam scared Microsoft so much that the corporation offered him a programmer's job.*

■■■ *In 1981, Ian Murphy, known to his friends as Captain Zap, achieved the distinction of being* **the first hacker to be convicted on felony charges.** *He hacked into U.S. phone company AT&T and changed the clocks, allowing people to get late-night discounts at midday, but higher rates when they called at night.*

■■■ *A Canadian kid calling himself MafiaBoy launched a denial-of-service attack that* **crippled many of the Internet's largest sites**, *including Amazon, eBay and Yahoo, in the same week in February 2000.*

▪▪▪ *A group of hackers posted a* **bogus report on the PBS website** *in 2011 claiming that U.S. rappers Tupac Shakur and Biggie Smalls, who were shot dead in 1996 and 1997 respectively, were really alive and well and living in New Zealand.*

Death by 9V battery The static shock from a doorknob can exceed 10,000 volts, but although that sounds impressive, static electricity has such a low current as to render it harmless. However, a 9-volt battery can kill you, as an unfortunate U.S. Navy sailor discovered to his cost. Keen to test the resistance level of the human body, he picked up a battery-powered multimeter and took a probe in each hand to measure his resistance from thumb to thumb. Alas, he decided to take the experiment a stage further and find out what would happen if he let the probe's sharp tips break the skin of his thumbs. With his blood now acting as a conducting fluid, the current from the multimeter shot straight across his heart, killing him before he had a chance to record his findings.

The vomit beam A U.S. company has developed a weapon that can shoot an invisible beam through walls to incapacitate everyone in a room. The makers claim it produces disorientation, confusion and "extreme motion sickness"—vomiting to you and me—adding that the weapon could be used by the military to disable (but not injure) individuals in urban combat settings, such as hostage situations.

Misplaced nuclear weapons

During the Cold War, the United States military misplaced at least eight nuclear weapons permanently—a combined explosive force 2,200 times the Hiroshima bomb.

① *February 13, 1950*
Engine failure forced a B-36 bomber on a training flight to jettison its cargo—a 30-kiloton nuclear bomb—over the Pacific Ocean. The conventional explosives detonated on impact, but the bomb's uranium components were never recovered.

② and **③** *March 10, 1956*
A B-47 carrying two nuclear weapon cores vanished in thick cloud over the Mediterranean Sea. Neither the plane nor its cargo was ever found.

④ and **⑤** *January 24, 1961*
A B-52 carrying two 24-megaton nuclear bombs crashed while taking off from an airbase in Goldsboro, North Carolina. One of the weapons sank in a swamp and its uranium core was never found.

⑥ *December 5, 1965*
An A-4E Skyhawk plane carrying a hydrogen bomb fell off the deck of the aircraft carrier USS Ticonderoga *off the Pacific coast of Japan and sank in 16,000 ft (4,876 m) of water, never to be seen again.*

7 and **8** c.22 May, 1968

Returning to its base in Norfolk, Virginia, nuclear attack submarine USS Scorpion sank 400 miles (644 km) southwest of the Azores, losing all 99 crew members and its two unspecified nuclear weapons.

A devastating solar storm could wipe out Earth's technology—and experts say one's coming soon NASA scientists have warned that a giant explosion of energy from the Sun—unleashed with the force of 1,000 atomic bombs—could paralyze the Earth in 2013, knocking out power, destroying technology, shutting down the Internet, crippling communication satellites and causing global chaos. In effect, it could take us back—for a decade at least—to the 18th century. The Sun will reach a critical stage of its cycle in 2013, with a blast of magnetic energy in its atmosphere likely to trigger radiation storms that will cause massive power surges.

The last big solar flare, in 1859, covered two-thirds of the Earth's skies in a blood-red aurora. The skies were so bright that miners in the Rocky Mountains started cooking breakfast in the middle of the night because they thought it was morning. Miles of telegraph lines were burned out across the U.S. and Europe, although at the height of the solar storm the lines between Boston and Portland that were not completely destroyed worked for hours using only power from the storm. In 1989, a smaller solar storm took just 90 seconds to knock out power to six million people in Canada, which was good news for candle sellers but nobody else. The damage cost hundreds of millions of dollars and took months to repair. If the forecasts are correct, 2013 could be much, much worse.

Japanese gaming giant Nintendo was founded in 1889—and they started by making playing cards.

Britain's nuclear chicken bomb During the Cold War, the British Ministry of Defence planned to fill a buried nuclear landmine with live chickens to ensure that it stayed at the correct temperature. Information about this idea was eventually released on April 1, 2004, but officials maintained that the date was pure coincidence. One commented, "The Civil Service does not do jokes."

Robots can learn to lie to each other In a worrying development, robots in a Swiss laboratory have been taught to lie and starve each other. The 1,000 robots each had a blue light that they were trained to turn on when they found a food source at the end of the testing room, thereby alerting their fellow robots to the location of the food. However, there were limited spaces at the food source, meaning that a robot informing others of its whereabouts might lose out. The best-performing robots were allowed to "mate" with each other, passing on their information to the next generation—but within 500 generations more than half of the robots had learned to keep their blue lights off upon finding the food. Some robots even seemed attracted to the liars with non-illuminated lights, sensing that they were hiding something worthwhile. You just can't trust anyone these days.

The fax machine came before the telephone Believe it or not, the fax machine was invented as far back as 1843 by Scotsman Alexander Bain—33 years before Alexander Bell came up with the telephone.

The slinky toy was originally invented as part of a battleship In 1943, naval engineer Richard James was working with tension springs as he tried to develop a meter designed to monitor horsepower on battleships. When one of the springs fell to the ground, he noticed how the spring kept moving after it landed and thought it would make the basis for a great toy.

Franz Reichelt's ingenious flying overcoat, which failed horribly Nine years after the Wright brothers first took to the skies, Frenchman Franz Reichelt used his skills as a tailor to create a giant overcoat, which he was convinced would allow him to fly or at least glide to the ground. To test his theory, he jumped 197 ft (60 m) from the first deck of the Eiffel Tower in 1912—and plunged like a stone to his death. Contemporary film of the hapless attempt at manned flight shows the hole his body made in the ground upon impact.

"Mad scientist" Nikola Tesla predicted the Blackberry in 1902, and was working on a death ray when he died Writing over a century ago in the magazine *Popular Mechanics*, the Serbian-born physicist predicted that one day it would be possible to send wireless messages all over the world by means of a hand-held device, and that everyone in the world would use it to communicate with friends. Toward the end of his life, in 1943, Tesla was working on a death ray supposedly capable of bringing down a fleet of 10,000 airplanes from a distance of 250 miles (400 km). He tried to sell the weapon to a number of countries—including the U.S.—but none would take it. Some 20 years earlier, an English inventor, Harry Grindell Matthews, also claimed to have devised an invisible death ray. He said his demon beam could shoot down airplanes, explode gunpowder, stop ships and motorcycles, and incapacitate infantry from four miles away. He occasionally demonstrated the ray privately to journalists, but refused to explain how it worked and ultimately failed to convince any government of its authenticity. One of his next inventions was to project a picture of an angel onto a cloud with a Christmas greeting. He was nothing if not versatile.

❝invisible death ray❞

Could someone turn off the Internet? A new cyberweapon could take down the entire Internet—and according to Max Schuchard at the University of Minnesota, there's not much that current defenses could do to stop it. The attack, which would pit the structure of the Internet against itself, requires a large botnet—a network of computers infected with software that allows them to be controlled externally. Schuchard reckons 250,000 such machines would be sufficient to turn off the Internet around the world.

China's electronics graveyard The small Guiyu region of China—covering just four villages—is the biggest electronics waste site in the world, with around 150,000 workers sorting the 100 truckloads that are dumped there every day. The pollution risks to the workers are enormous, with nearly 90% suffering ill health. The local water is undrinkable, and the level of lead in the blood of Guiyu's children is over 50% higher than in children in surrounding areas. China as a whole receives an estimated one million tons of electronic waste every year, principally from the U.S., Canada and Japan.

The secret U.S. nuclear launch codes were reportedly set at "00000000" for 16 years during the Cold War.

Woman accidentally cuts off nation's Internet While scavenging for copper to sell as scrap, a 75-year-old Georgian woman sliced through an underground fiber-optic cable and cut off Internet access to the whole of Armenia for five hours. Large parts of Georgia, which provides 90% of Armenia's Internet, and Azerbaijan were also affected.

Secret Service gadgets

▪▪▪ Poison umbrella

A seemingly innocuous umbrella that fired a deadly poison pellet from its tip, in this case ricin, was used to kill Bulgarian dissident writer Georgi Markov in London in 1978.

▪▪▪ Pipe pistol

For the gentleman assassin, the British pipe pistol was the perfect companion to the poison umbrella. It was fired by twisting the pipe bowl while holding the stem.

▪▪▪ Compass buttons

If a British agent became lost or was captured during World War II, he could cut off the specially magnetized fly buttons on his pants, balance them on top of each other and they turned into a compass to help him find a way out of his predicament.

▪▪▪ Miniature spy plane

During the 1970s, the CIA developed the first UAV (Unmanned Aerial Vehicle)—the insectothopter—a miniature flying surveillance device in the shape of a dragonfly.

▪▪▪ Microdot camera

The microdot camera was an invaluable CIA weapon in the Cold War, being able to photograph and condense pages of information onto a tiny piece of film the size of a sentence period. The film could then be embedded into otherwise mundane correspondence as punctuation at the end of a sentence.

▪▪▪ Lipstick gun

For the female spy, the KGB produced a lethal lipstick gun that delivered the kiss of death with a single 4.5-mm shot.

▪▪▪ Tear gas pen

MI6's Q branch developed a range of ingenious gadgets for spies, including a pen that fired tear gas, cigarettes drugged with cocaine (when available) and an exploding safe to get rid of secret documents.

▪▪▪ Secret coins

The CIA used to hollow out silver dollar coins to conceal messages or film.

▪▪▪ Olive bug

Ideal for placing inside a vodka Martini, the olive bug, as demonstrated in the U.S. in the 1960s, was a fake olive that contained a miniature microphone. The toothpick served as an antenna to achieve a bugging range of about 30 ft (9 m).

▪▪▪ Cyanide specs

Preferring to die than be tortured, a captured spy could chew on the tip of a pair of CIA-issue spectacles to reach the deadly cyanide pellet concealed inside.

Computers are getting bigger, not smaller The first multi-purpose computer, IBM's "Giant Brain," the U.S. Army's Electronic Numerical Integrator And Computer (ENIAC), was unveiled in 1946, and was one thousand times more powerful than its predecessors. To create all this processing power, it needed 17,478 vacuum tubes, enough power to run a modern American home for a week (it was about the same size physically!) and it weighed as much as two school buses. Although you might think computers have become steadily smaller since then, China's Tianhe-1a, the fastest computer in the world today, takes up almost ten times more space than ENIAC, and is six times heavier, requiring power equivalent to running 25 U.S. houses for a week. However, it is around 500,000 times more powerful than the basic home PC.

❝weighed as much as two school buses❞

Ronald Mallett's time machine University of Connecticut professor Ronald Mallett has used the equations of Einstein's relativity theories to design a time machine with circulating laser beams. He is confident that at some point in the 21st century—maybe even by 2016—people will be able to travel in time using this method. He was inspired by the death of his father at age 33 from a heart attack, and resolved to find a way of traveling back in time so that he could warn him about the dangers of smoking.

Man tries to sell son on Craigslist There are times when we've all probably thought about it, but a Washington man actually did put his four-year-old son up for sale on Craigslist, at an asking price of $5,000. The ad said that the boy "loves playing with balls" but "refuses to eat vegetables. He doesn't fuss very much but when he does he just screams for hours. I usually just put him in the closet until he stops and that usually works."

Robots fool thousands of Twitter followers Three groups unleashed software that pretends to be human and used it to fool Twitter users into thinking that they were real people. Over a two-week period, the three socialbots received numerous replies to their tweets and picked up nearly 250 followers between them.

News of actress Anne Hathaway might correlate with the stock price of Warren Buffett's Berkshire Hathaway company It seems that whenever actress Anne Hathaway is in the news online, the stock price of Warren Buffett's Berkshire Hathaway company goes up. On six separate occasions over a two-year period, the "Hathaway effect," as it has become known, saw a significant rise in BH stock price whenever AH had a new film premiere. One explanation is that automated trading programming is picking up the same chatter on the Internet about "Hathaway" as the International Movie Data Base's star meter, and is applying it to the stock market.

Extreme gamers

▪▪▪ *A Chinese man died in 2011 after a* **three-day nonstop gaming session** *during which he barely ate. He lost consciousness at a Beijing Internet café, having apparently spent $1,500 on gaming in the month leading up to his death.*

▪▪▪ *A 28-year-old South Korean died of heart failure stemming from exhaustion after* **playing *Starcraft* for 50 hours** *in an Internet café.*

▪▪▪ *A 13-year-old Chinese gaming addict threw himself off the 24th floor of an apartment tower, having written his* **suicide note through the eyes of a video game character**.

▪▪▪ *A South Korean couple were convicted of negligent homicide after their baby starved while they spent* **up to 12 hours a day in Internet cafés** *raising a virtual child online.*

▪▪▪ *A Chinese man was* **stabbed to death in a row over a sword in the online game *Legends of Mir 3*.** *Qiu Chengwei lent fellow gamer Zhu Caoyuan his powerful virtual sword, Dragon Sabre, but when Zhu sold the sword on eBay for $870, Qiu took real-world revenge.*

▪▪▪ World of Warcraft *players can buy or sell weapons and armor to make their characters more powerful. The game's currency is gold, which is earned by doing jobs like mining or collecting herbs, but because these tasks are so time-consuming, websites now offer to sell the virtual gold that might have taken 100 hours to collect for around $30 in real money. To obtain that gold, companies in China have been set up where* **people work for up to 12 hours a day to "farm" gold from the game** *by carrying out the menial chores.*

▪▪▪ *Craig Smallwood of Hawaii sued the gaming company NCsoft for negligence for not explaining to him that their game* Lineage II *could be addictive. He said he had* **played the game for 20,000 hours** *between 2004 and 2009 and would never have started if he had realized he would become hooked. He added that as a result of his addiction he is "unable to function independently in usual daily activities."*

▪▪▪ *A Japanese man became so* **infatuated with the character Nene Anegasaki from the Nintendo DS game** *Love Plus that he married her in a solemn ceremony in Tokyo. The groom, who calls himself SAL9000, read his vows before the bride flashed hers up on the screen of his DS, which was being held by the best man. SAL said he fell in love with Nene after a string of failed romances with girlfriends from other video games.*

▪▪▪ *There are 11.5 million* World of Warcraft *players in the world, more than the population of Belgium. One* World of Warcraft *player* **sold an avatar account for $9,900.**

▪▪▪ Second Life *player Ailin Graef from China has become* **a real-world millionaire through her avatar Anshe Chung.** *Graef has calculated her worth based on Chung's extensive property portfolio and other business interests, which can be converted from the game's currency, Linden dollars, to real cash.*

▪▪▪ *Yan Panasjuk, a software engineer from Boston, Massachusetts,* **paid $335,000 in real money** *to Jon Jacobs for his online* Entropia *destination Club Neverdie. Why would anyone pay that much for something that only exists in a virtual world? Because* Entropia *is an online game where players can exchange Project Entropia dollars for real U.S. dollars at a 10:1 exchange rate.*

Chinese teenager sells kidney for iPad A 17-year-old Chinese boy sold one of his kidneys online for $3,000 so that he could buy the new iPad 2. Surfing the Internet, he spotted an advert offering money to organ donors, so he traveled north to the city of Chenzhou, where the kidney was removed at a local hospital. The first his mother knew about the deal was when he returned home with a laptop, an iPad and a livid red scar.

British intelligence attacks al-Qaeda with cupcakes Britain's MI6 hacked into an al-Qaeda online magazine in 2011 and substituted deadly bomb-making instructions with recipes for cupcakes. When followers tried to download the magazine's article about making a lethal pipe bomb in the kitchen, they found instead a garbled computer code, inserted by British intelligence hackers, which revealed a web page of recipes for "The Best Cupcakes in America" published by the Ellen DeGeneres chat show.

Goooooooooooooooooooooooooooooooooooooooooooooooooooo ooooooooooooooooooooooooooooooooooooooooooooooooooooo ooooogle. There are 100 zeros in a Googol, or ten duotrigintillion, the number that inspired Google.

Mark Zuckerberg had his Facebook account deleted—Mark S. Zuckerberg, that is Sometimes having a famous name can be a curse. Just ask Indianapolis bankruptcy attorney Mark S.

Zuckerberg, who had his Facebook account disabled because the social networking site thought he was lying about his name and spoofing Facebook founder Mark E. Zuckerberg. Mark S. said that when he first signed up on Facebook, he had to send additional proof of identity—including his birth certificate and bar association license—before he was allowed to join.

Carrier pigeon or Internet—which is faster? A race took place in South Africa recently between a carrier pigeon and a broadband Internet provider. Who transferred a data package the fastest?

a The pigeon
b The broadband Internet
c Neither

[Answer:

a *The pigeon—The bird took 1 hour 8 minutes to fly the 50 miles (80 km) from Pietermaritzburg to Durban with a data card strapped to its leg—and including download, the transfer took just over two hours. In that time only 4% of the data had been transferred over the Internet.]*

You can buy pieces of New York garbage on the Internet as a souvenir Since 2001, Justin Gignac has been selling online pieces of authentic New York City garbage, encased in transparent plastic, smell-proof cubes and signed and dated by the artist himself, for $50 apiece. To date, he's sold over 1,300.

Using new laser technology, it is now possible to transfer digitally the entire U.S. Library of Congress collection in 10 seconds.

The groom who changed his Facebook status at the altar Partway through his 2009 wedding ceremony, computer programmer Dana Hanna of Abingdon, Maryland, pulled out his BlackBerry and not only changed his relationship status to "married" on Facebook but also sent out a tweet announcing that he and Tracy Page had just married... all before he kissed the bride. That's what is called getting your priorities right.

A Norwegian festival attracts thousands of young people, and they all bring their computers Every Easter, over 5,000 young people converge on the Vikingskipet Olympic Arena in Hamar, Norway, for a five-day festival with a difference. The Gathering is the world's largest computer party, and the festival-goers are there to play online games.

Online dating taken to extremes (the girlfriend is virtual) Just when you thought relationships couldn't get any more complicated, Facebook hosts a new dating site on which your dream girlfriend is exactly that—a dream. Cloud Girlfriend aims to fill in that gap in your life by creating your perfect virtual girlfriend. You simply tell the site what makes your ideal girl, and before you know it you are enjoying a virtual long-distance relationship with her. It is hoped that the experience will eventually help users to manage a genuine relationship, and that they will be able to take what they have learned into the real world.

The "Demon Core" plutonium used for the Bikini Atoll nuclear bombs claimed the lives of two U.S. scientists on separate occasions before it was even used In August 1945, physicist Harry Daghlian was working alone on a 14-lb (6.3-kg) spherical mass of plutonium at the Los Alamos Laboratory, New Mexico. While attempting to stack another tungsten carbide brick around the assembly, he accidentally dropped it into the core, causing the core to go critical. Although the core didn't explode, Daghlian died from radiation poisoning 28 days later.

Then, in May 1946, physicist Louis Slotin and seven other scientists at Los Alamos were conducting a dangerous experiment that involved creating the first steps of a nuclear fission reactor by placing two half-spheres of beryllium around the plutonium core. The trick, which Slotin called "tickling the dragon's tail," was to prevent the beryllium from touching the plutonium core. Slotin had performed the procedure many times before, but on this occasion his screwdriver slipped a fraction of an inch and the beryllium hemisphere touched the core, which instantly went critical. There was a flash of blue light, followed by a wave of heat across Slotin's skin. Realizing his error, he immediately lifted the beryllium with his hand, but it was enough to give him a fatal dose of radiation, from which he died nine days later. Three of the other scientists present later died from the side effects of radiation. The plutonium core was subsequently nicknamed the "Demon Core" and was put to use just five weeks after the second incident in the Operator Crossroads nuclear weapon test at Bikini Atoll. Coincidentally, both incidents took place on Tuesday the 21st and both men died in the same room at the same hospital.

A woman in Tennessee was arrested on the grounds that she had violated a legal order of protection that had been filed against her by "poking" another woman on Facebook.

When unbreakable glass isn't unbreakable Toronto lawyer Garry Hoy repeatedly demonstrated the "unbreakable" glass in his office building by jumping into it, until it broke. Hoy was proud of the toughened glass in the high-rise Toronto-Dominion Center. He loved to demonstrate how unbreakable the glass

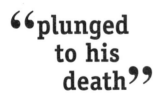

"plunged to his death" windows were by hurling his body against them, and his fellow lawyers were always impressed when he bounced off harmlessly. Until July 9, 1993, that is.

On that day, Hoy performed his party piece to a group of law students in the boardroom, but the glass gave way and he plunged 24 floors to his death.

The boy who tried to use a chat room to get himself killed
A 15-year-old British schoolboy was convicted of inciting an Internet friend to murder him. The boy, known only as John, had fallen in love with an older boy, Mark, and adopted the guise of a female secret service agent on a chat room so that "she" could order Mark to stab him in a Cheshire alleyway in 2004. Agent 47695, as she was known, instructed Mark to kill John, promising him as a reward a gun, a large sum of money and a meeting with the then British Prime Minister Tony Blair. Mark went ahead with the stabbing, but John survived the attack. The boys initially claimed a stranger in black had been responsible, but police uncovered the truth by studying 58,000 lines of Internet text to reveal that John had spent six months manipulating Mark until he felt he was ready to commit murder.

More than two days' worth of video clips are uploaded to YouTube every minute.

A White House sense of humor "Rickrolling" is an Internet phenomenon in which an unsuspecting user who clicks on a link is directed to the video of Rick Astley's 1987 hit "Never Gonna Give You Up." One such user was David Wiggs from Tennessee who complained, in July 2011, that the White House Twitter feed on U.S. debt was dull. The White House duly "rickrolled" him by suggesting he click on the link that led straight to Astley's video.

Sceptic challenges guru to kill him live on TV When tantric guru Pandit Surender Sharma boasted on an Indian TV talk show that he could kill a man within three minutes using only his mystical powers, disbeliever Sanal Edamaruku said bluntly, "Go on then—kill me." Sharma was at first reluctant to take up the challenge but eventually agreed to perform a series of rituals designed to kill Mr. Edamaruku on live television—a sure-fire ratings winner if ever there was one. The guru began by chanting 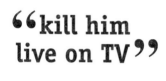 mantras, then he sprinkled water on Mr. Edamaruku before waving a knife and then ruffling the sceptic's hair. This went on for several hours, but his intended victim remained very much alive, smiling for the cameras and mocking the increasingly agitated holy man. Desperate to save face, Sharma accused him of praying to the gods for protection, but Mr. Edamaruku replied that he was an atheist. Finally, Sharma resorted to foul play, pressing his thumbs hard enough against Mr Edamaruku's temples to kill him in a conventional manner until the show's anchor ordered him to stop. So, the guru claimed that he needed to conduct an elaborate ritual that had to be done at night, outdoors, and only after he had slept with a woman, drunk alcohol, eaten meat and rubbed his body in ash. The two men agreed to go to an outdoor studio that night, where Sharma, surrounded by flames, white smoke, a voodoo doll and a chorus of chanters, tried once more to kill his adversary, but still to no avail. At midnight, the anchor finally declared it was game over. Sceptic 1: Mystic 0.

Brad Pitt is banned from ever entering China because of his role in the movie *Seven Years in Tibet*.

The $10-million book A copy of John James Audubon's 1830s' masterpiece *Birds of America*—one of only 119 in existence—sold for $10.3 million in 2010. With giant pages measuring 39 x 26 in (100 x 67 cm), it was printed in double elephant folio to allow life-size illustration of birds. Audubon is viewed today as a great conservationist—ironic considering that, in order to paint the birds accurately, he first killed them.

What produces the lowest note ever found in the Universe? Astronomers in the U.S. have detected a note emitted from a massive black hole 250 million light-years away and have calculated it as B flat. We won't be able to hear it, however, as it is 57 octaves lower than middle C, at a frequency over a million, billion times deeper than the limits of human hearing.

The book bound in human skin An 1852 poetry book containing the works of *Paradise Lost* poet John Milton hides a gruesome fact—it is bound with the skin of a convicted murderer. George Cudmore's body was stripped of its flesh shortly after he was hanged for killing his lover in Exeter, England, and a portion of his skin ended up in the hands of a local bookseller who used it to bind Milton's work.

Life imitates the movies

▪▪▪ The China Syndrome (U.S. 1979)

The story of two journalists (played by Michael Douglas and Jane Fonda) who uncover safety issues at a nuclear power plant, the movie was roundly criticized as irresponsible scaremongering by the nuclear power industry. Just 12 days after the film's release, the Three Mile Island nuclear power plant in Pennsylvania suffered a partial meltdown, resulting in widespread panic and an evacuation of the surrounding area. Capitalizing on the similarities, The China Syndrome *cleaned up at the box office.*

▪▪▪ Americathon (U.S. 1979)

Starring John Ritter and Harvey Korman, Americathon *predicted that 20 years into the future the U.S.S.R. would collapse, China would become a global economic superpower and the U.S. would be deep in debt. It also forecast that Nike, then a fledgling shoe company in Oregon, would become a multinational conglomerate, people would drink expensive, specialty coffee, smoking would be banned and reality TV would reach absurd limits.*

▪▪▪ Back to the Future Part II (U.S. 1989)

This sci-fi movie predicted that the average family would one day have at least one big flat-screen TV with hundreds of channels—a seemingly far-fetched view of how we might watch TV in the future.

■■□ **Office Space** (U.S. 1999)

In this comedy, the lead character scams his employer by shaving pennies off a large number of transactions. In 2009, a 22-year-old computer programmer pulled a similar stunt when he set up tens of thousands of accounts with financial companies and pocketed the test deposits, usually only a few pennies. Officials may have been alerted by the fact that he opened the accounts in the names of famous cartoon characters.

■■□ **Inside Man** (U.S. 2006)

A bank robber in London, inspired by Clive Owen's character in this heist movie, wore a boiler suit and came armed with spares, which he handed out to the 16 bank staff he took hostage in order to conceal his identity.

Ltester in wrods cna be rerargnaed adn yuo cna siltl udnretsnad wtha tyhe maen Why? Because of the way our brain processes language, we can easily read jumbled words provided the first and, in the case of long words, the last letters are in the right order.

The Nepalese cursing festival The young people of two neighboring villages in Nepal take part in an annual ten-day cursing festival, where they hurl their choicest insults at one another—such as, "Monkey face, I hope your sons are as ugly as frogs" and "I hope your buffaloes die of diarrhea."

Movie trivia

■■■ *The famous scene in* **Taxi Driver** *(U.S. 1976) where Travis Bickle (Robert De Niro) is talking to himself in the mirror was completely ad-libbed. It was never in the script, but is drawn from an exercise used by acting teachers where the students are told to repeat the same phrase over and over again, putting the emphasis on a different word each time to convey a new meaning. De Niro learned the technique under legendary New York acting teacher Stella Adler.*

■■■ *The mechanical shark in* **Jaws** *(U.S. 1975) was named Bruce after director Steven Spielberg's lawyer.*

■■■ *Roger Moore suffers from hoplophobia, a fear of firearms, which meant that a number of his scenes as James Bond had to be re-shot. Being* **The Man with the Golden Gun** *(U.K. 1974) gave him a nervous tic because as soon as he picked up a gun, he started to blink uncontrollably.*

■■■ *The biblical passage in* **Pulp Fiction** *(U.S. 1994) is only very loosely based on the Bible—most of it was made up by Quentin Tarantino and Samuel L. Jackson.*

■■■ *The slow-motion scene at the end of* **Carrie** *(U.S. 1976) was filmed in reverse to simulate ghostlike movement. If you look closely at the top left-hand corner of the screen, you can see cars being driven backward.*

▪▪▪ *Crime boss Joseph Columbo Sr. offered to help with the filming of* **The Godfather** *(U.S. 1972), provided the script did not include the word "mafia." It was an offer the producers couldn't refuse. When actor James Caan met gangster Carmine "The Snake" Persico to research his role in the film, undercover FBI agents mistook him for an up-and-coming gangster and kept an eye on them both.*

▪▪▪ *Brooke Shields spent much of* **The Blue Lagoon** *(U.S. 1980) standing in a trench beside Christopher Atkins so that she wouldn't appear taller than him in their scenes together. Although she was only 14 at the time and he was 18, at 5 ft 10 in (1.8 m) she towered over him by 4 in (10 cm).*

▪▪▪ *The title of the 1968 movie* **Krakatoa, East of Java** *(U.S. 1969) is geographically inaccurate—Krakatoa was 200 miles (320 km) west of Java.*

▪▪▪ *The real-life Baron von Franckenstein, a professional actor, appeared in* **Young Frankenstein** *(U.S. 1974) under his screen name Clement St. George, but did not play his namesake.*

A serious book on international relations—and zombies

Daniel W. Drezner, a professor of international politics, has written a scholarly book in which he envisages how various national governments and the United Nations would respond to a zombie invasion. Mr. Drezner is said to be big on zombies.

The man who didn't catch a bullet To add a touch of oriental mystique to his act, American magician William Ellsworth Robinson adopted the stage name Chung Ling Soo and maintained the illusion of being Chinese by never speaking onstage and always talking to journalists via an interpreter. For his most spectacular trick, his assistants took two guns to the stage and members of the audience were asked to mark the bullets that were loaded into the guns. The assistants then fired at Chung, who appeared to catch the bullets in his teeth and spit them out onto a plate. In truth, he had secretly hidden the marked bullets in his hand, and the guns were rigged so that live ammunition was never actually fired. Instead, the flash from the pan was channeled to a blank charge in the ramrod tube beneath the barrel. There was a bang, the audience was impressed and Chung always lived to perform another day. But one night in London, England, in 1918, the trick backfired tragically and proved to be Chung Ling Soo's final curtain call. Since the gun had never been unloaded properly, over a period of time a residue of unburned gunpowder had built up in the channel that allowed the flash to bypass the barrel and ignite the charge in the ramrod tube. On the fateful night, the flash from the pan instead ignited the charge behind the real bullet in the barrel of one of the guns. The bullet hit Chung in the chest. Dropping his Chinese persona in public for the first and last time, he muttered, "Oh my God! I've been shot. Lower the curtain!" He died the next day, leaving his poor wife to reveal to the inquest how the trick worked on a good night. The gun that killed Chung now resides in David Copperfield's collection of magic memorabilia.

The cello scrotum hoax A leading doctor hoodwinked the *British Medical Journal* for 30 years after inventing a medical condition called "cello scrotum." Elaine Murphy—now Baroness Murphy—came up with the idea in the 1970s after reading about a phenomenon called "guitar nipple," reportedly caused by the edge of the guitar pressing against the breast. So, she decided to create a similar affliction for cellists—and not only was the letter published, but "cello scrotum" was subsequently referenced on several occasions over the ensuing decades by the *BMJ* and other medical journals. One scholar went so far as to debate whether it was awkward contact with the chair, rather than with the instrument, that caused the irritation.

By April 2011, U2's *360°* tour had grossed $558 million, more than the gross domestic product of Samoa.

The first April Fools In 1983, Professor Joseph Boskin of Boston University revealed the ancient origin of April Fool's Day to a journalist. According to Boskin, the 5th-century Roman Emperor Constantine was told by one of his court jesters that fools could rule the Roman Empire more effectively. Constantine took the joke well, and gave the jesters one day in which they could indeed govern the Empire. The head of jesters, named Kugel, decreed that only the absurd was allowed to happen on that day—and so the April Fool tradition was born. The story went out on the Associated Press wire and was printed by many large newspapers as a serious plea for more humor in society.

What was the date that the story broke? April 1. Professor Boskin had made the whole story up and managed to successfully prank the nation.

Less amusing were the "jokes" played by dictator Saddam Hussein and his sons in Iraq. Uday Hussein owned a newspaper, which reported cruel lies for a number of years on April Fool's Day, including front page news that tough United Nations sanctions against Iraq would be lifted by President Clinton, that food rations would soon include cola drinks and chocolate, that embargoed BMW cars would soon be arriving, and that all students would automatically pass their exams that year. After Saddam Hussein's removal, it was also reported that a U.S. spy, working undercover as a diplomat and codenamed "April Fools," fed Iraqi intelligence false plans for an American invasion from Jordan, leaving the real U.S. invasion route, from Turkey, clear of Iraqi troops.

Sacha Baron Cohen's film *The Dictator* is based on a novel reportedly written by real-life dictator Saddam Hussein, a romantic story named *Zabibah and the King*.

A convicted murderer helped write the first dictionary
William Chester Minor, a former U.S. Army surgeon, was vital to the development of the first *Oxford English Dictionary*. He compiled thousands of phrases to match up to every word in the dictionary—and had time to do this because he was imprisoned for murder in a psychiatric hospital.

Composer Nathan Currier accused the Brooklyn Philhar-
monic Orchestra of stopping partway through the 2004
premiere of his magnum opus *Gaian Variations* to avoid
paying its musicians overtime.

The great Shakespeare hoax Shakespearean artifacts were
big business in 18th-century England. Over 100 years after
his death, Shakespeare was acknowledged as a true genius,
and the country was gripped by Bard fever as the literati
sought desperately to learn more about the great man and,
in particular, to unearth any material written in his own
hand. Among the devotees was an elderly London bookseller
named Samuel Ireland, who had collected a handful of relics
from Shakespeare's birthplace at Stratford-upon-Avon but
was eager for more. Samuel had a son, William Henry Ireland,
whose literary pretensions were bluntly dismissed by his father.
Samuel had little time for William and even hinted that he was
not really his son at all. One day in 1794, William, then 19,
hit upon a way of getting into his father's good books. Finding
some old parchment, he copied Shakespeare's signature and
presented it to his father as a title deed to a property. When
the forged signature was declared genuine by an expert, Samuel
was overjoyed.

Buoyed by his success, William produced further "finds"—a
forged letter of appreciation to Shakespeare from Queen
Elizabeth I and a bogus love poem from Shakespeare to his wife,
Anne Hathaway—which went on display in Samuel Ireland's
shop and drew visitors from far and wide, including the Prince

of Wales and revered biographer James Boswell. The praise for these "masterpieces" quickly went to William's head. Next he announced that he had uncovered the original manuscripts of *Hamlet* and *King Lear*, and, not content with reproducing the plays in an imitation of Shakespeare's hand, he made what he considered to be his own improvements to the text.

Having seen his forged letters and poems accepted as the genuine article, William embarked on his most ambitious undertaking to date—a full-length Shakespearean work. He told his father he had found the manuscript of a previously undiscovered five-act Shakespeare play, *Vortigern and Rowena*, based on the life of an Anglo-Saxon king. Amid much excitement, the world premiere of *Vortigern and Rowena* was to be performed at

❝the opening night was a disaster❞

London's Drury Lane Theatre in the spring of 1796, but by then Ireland's discoveries were beginning to be questioned. Edmond Malone, a leading expert, became highly suspicious of their authenticity, not least because the supposed letter from Queen Elizabeth I to Shakespeare referred to the anticipated presence of the Earl of Leicester at the famous Globe Theatre—even though Leicester had died six years before The Globe opened.

Unfortunately for Ireland, John Kemble, the producer of *Vortigern and Rowena*, shared Malone's misgivings and seemed to do his best to sabotage the play. The opening night—before 2,500 people—was a disaster. Kemble had given a role requiring immense gravitas to an actor with a distinctly high-pitched voice, as a result of which his every utterance provoked howls of laughter from the audience. Imagine Liberace playing Conan the Barbarian. Then a Saxon soldier died in the wrong place and became painfully trapped beneath the curtain as the scene ended. While the "corpse" tried to free himself from his ignominy, a drunk climbed on stage to lend a helping hand and was pelted with oranges. The final curtain almost produced a riot. There was no second night.

The farce, coupled with Malone's revelations, left few in any doubt that William's works were fakes. No doubt anxious to preserve his own reputation, for once Samuel Ireland defended his son, maintaining that he wasn't talented enough to have carried out such a complex fraud. That insult was the last straw for William, who had just completed a second Shakespeare play, *Henry II*, and had also started writing *William the Conqueror*. He came clean and publicly confessed that he had faked everything. His father never spoke to him again, but insisted right up until his death in 1803 that *Vortigern and Rowena* was a genuine Shakespeare play. Meanwhile, William went to live in France where he wrote over a dozen novels and plays, proving that he did have a real literary talent. Alas, by then it was too late to impress his father.

▮▮▮

The Rolling Stones' drummer Charlie Watts draws every bed he sleeps in With 147 dates on the band's most recent tour—and he has been keeping this "diary" since 1968—that amounts to rather a lot of beds.

Abscotchalater
one who is hiding from the police

Boondoggle
a scheme that wastes time and money

Crapulous
sick from too much drinking

Honeyfuggle
to dupe, deceive, swindle

Honorificabilitudinitatibus
honorableness—it was good enough for Shakespeare who used it in Love's Labour's Lost

Macroverbumsciolist
1. a person who is ignorant of long words
2. a person who pretends to know a word, then secretly refers to a dictionary

Pneumonoultramicroscopicsilicovolcanoconiosis
a lung disease caused by inhaling volcanic ash. At 45 letters, it's the longest word in the Oxford English Dictionary. *By the time the doctor has told you what you're suffering from, you'll probably be dead.*

Quakebuttock
a coward

Quidnunckery

curiosity, love of news or gossip

Rumbledethumps

a Scottish dish of potato and cabbage

Sesquipedalianist

one who uses overly long words

Snollygoster

an unprincipled person, especially a politician

Spelunking

cave exploration

Vomitorium

the exit from a Roman theater (no vomit was involved)

Was Dr. Frankenstein based on a real person? Mary Shelley's inspiration may well have been the Johann Dippel, a 17th-century alchemist who actually lived in Castle Frankenstein, Germany. He devoted his life to discovering an elixir for immortality, and created "Dippel's Oil," a concoction made from bones, blood and other bodily fluids. He was also said to have been an ardent body snatcher, regularly stealing corpses from the local graveyard, and he wrote of his theory that the soul could be transferred from one body to another via a funnel.

FHM readers voted a man into their Top 100 sexiest women list Readers of *FHM* magazine slipped a "he" in among the "shes" for the 2011 list of the world's 100 sexiest women by voting androgynous Australian male model Andrej Pejic in 98th place, one place ahead of Lady Gaga.

In 1970, a top Japanese author committed seppuku—ritual samurai suicide Following a failed coup d'état, three-times Nobel Prize-nominated author Yukio Mishima committed seppuku, a traditional Japanese method of suicide by disembowelment then beheading. Considered a slightly more acceptable version of hara-kiri, it was originally practiced by samurai warriors so that they could die with honor rather than fall into the hands of the enemy. Mishima carried out the ritual by plunging a short blade into his abdomen and then moving it from left to right in a slicing movement. One of his fellow conspirators then beheaded him, but only after several failed attempts. It turned out that Mishima had been planning his spectacular suicide for at least a year, and that the attempted coup merely provided a platform for it.

Thirty years later, Dédé Fortin, singer with Canadian band Les Colocs, quietly committed suicide in his Montreal apartment also by seppuku. A friend found him lying in a pool of blood.

Tom Cruise has saved the lives of three people—one in Santa Monica, one off the island of Capri and one in London at the U.K. premiere of *Mission: Impossible.*

The most popular film ever, and you've probably never heard of it What is the most popular movie of all time? *Titanic*? *Lord of the Rings*? *Gone With the Wind*? No, it's a movie called *Jesus*, and although it has no Hollywood stars or big-name director, it has been seen by over two billion people across the world and translated into nearly 800 languages and dialects. Shot in the Holy Land in 1979, it is a straight retelling of the Gospel of St. Luke and owes its success to an American evangelical organization, Campus Crusade, whose members travel to far-flung corners of the world, showing screenings in improvised cinemas and distributing copies of the film wherever they can.

Author William S. Burroughs left a sample of his poop behind after he died in 1997 Now two artists want to clone the DNA, mix it with gold dust and shoot it from an air gun. Incredibly, it's true. Adam Zaretsky and Tony Allard plan to take a piece of Burroughs' preserved poop (it's covered in epoxy), isolate the DNA, make lots of copies of it, soak the DNA dust in gold dust, load it into a gun, then fire it into a mixture of blood, poop and semen and call it art. The tribute project has the full support of Burroughs' estate, the gun being an allusion to the incident in 1951 when Burroughs shot and killed his wife Joan while playing a drunken game of "William Tell."

Did you know Martin Scorsese directed Michael Jackson's *Bad* video?

Gruesome tales and rhymes

Some surprisingly gruesome original fairy tales that have been modified for modern children

- ▪▪▪ In the original story of *Little Red Riding Hood*, she is simply eaten by the wolf.

- ▪▪▪ In earlier versions of *Goldilocks*, she is either ripped apart by the three bears when they discover her in their house or she breaks her neck in a fall from a window while trying to escape.

- ▪▪▪ In the first version of Hans Christian Andersen's *The Little Mermaid*, the mermaid is so distraught at seeing the Prince marry someone else that she jumps into the ocean and dies by turning into froth.

- ▪▪▪ In the Brothers Grimm version of *Cinderella*, her stepsisters go to the trouble of chopping off parts of their feet to make the slipper fit.

- ▪▪▪ The Brothers Grimm again lived up to their name with their tale of *Snow White*, in which the wicked stepmother is tortured by being forced to wear red-hot iron shoes and made to dance until she drops down dead.

... and sinister origins of nursery rhymes

- ▪▪▪ The rhyme *"Mary, Mary, quite contrary"* actually details various methods of torture used during the reign of Queen Mary I of England in the 16th century.

- ▪▪▪ *"Three Blind Mice"* refers to the punishment handed out to three noblemen who conspired against the same Queen Mary of England. However, she didn't have them blinded and dismembered as in the rhyme—possibly because it hadn't occurred to her—but she did have them burnt at the stake.

- ▪▪▪ The *"Jack and Jill"* who went up the hill are King Louis XVI of France, who was guillotined ("lost his crown") during the French Revolution, and his Queen, Marie Antoinette, who suffered the same fate ("came tumbling after").

- ▪▪▪ The rhyme *"Oranges and Lemons"* describes the plight of prisoners on Death Row awaiting execution in 18th-century London.

- ▪▪▪ *"Georgie Porgie"* is George Villiers, Duke of Buckingham, the secret lover of King James I of England.

- ▪▪▪ *"Ring a Ring o' Roses"* had its origins in the Black Death, the deadly bubonic plague that swept through Europe in the 14th century. The last line, "atishoo, atishoo, we all fall down," refers to the sneezing that was the final fatal symptom.

The secret U.S. Army Hollywood division that risked their lives to film nuclear tests For decades, the U.S. Army kept secret the fact that a genuine division—known as the Lookout Mountain Laboratory—existed within Hollywood, which photographed and filmed more than 200 nuclear tests carried out by the military between 1947 and 1962. Surrounded by barbed wire, the building on Wonderland Avenue in Laurel Canyon had a sound stage, screening rooms and processing labs and housed around 250 people, including directors, producers and cameramen. The members of the unit put their lives on the line to produce around 6,500 films covering explosions in the Nevada Desert and the Pacific atolls, sometimes standing just two miles away from the blast. The material they captured provided valuable scientific information regarding the weapons' capacity for destruction and was also used to influence Congress with a view to continued funding. The blast from one detonation was so powerful it threw a photographer and his camera into a ditch. No sooner had he climbed back to his feet than a second wave knocked him down again. They didn't all live to tell the tale. Many died prematurely of cancer, almost certainly as a result of being subjected to large doses of radiation while filming. Sometimes their only protection against a 15-megaton bomb (the equivalent of over 1,100 Hiroshima bombs) was a baseball cap.

> **" filmed more than 200 nuclear tests "**

A 1938 edition of Action Comics No. 1—the first to feature Superman—sold in 2011 for over $2 million. It originally cost just 10¢ new.

Santiago Sierra's solid block of human excrement—is it art? Perhaps to prove there's art in all of us, Spanish-born artist Santiago Sierra staged an exhibition in London, England, consisting of 21, 7-ft-long (2.1-m) blocks of human excrement made from poop collected by scavengers in India.

Howard Hughes and the real Hollywood disaster movie Rated one of the worst movies of all time, *The Conqueror*—a 1956 production from the eccentric Howard Hughes and starring John Wayne—was a disaster in every respect. Filmed in Utah downwind from the U.S. government's Nevada nuclear testing site, it is believed the shoot contributed to the deaths of Wayne, co-stars Susan Hayward and Agnes Moorehead, and director Dick Powell, all of whom later died of cancer. Another member of the cast, Pedro Armendáriz, developed cancer of the kidney four years after filming and shot himself when he learned it was terminal. Of the cast and crew of 220, by 1981 a total of 91 had developed some form of cancer and 46 had died of the disease. Although nobody sued Hughes, he paid $12 million to withdraw *The Conqueror* from circulation by buying up every available copy, and until it was shown on TV in 1974 the only person who saw it was Hughes himself, who screened it night after night during the final, reclusive years of his life.

Banned films and TV shows

- ▪▪▫ *The Simpsons Movie* (U.S. 2007) was banned in Burma because the colors red and yellow aren't allowed in movies.

- ▪▪▫ The character **Mickey Mouse** was banned in Romania in 1935 on the grounds that a giant rodent would frighten children.

- ▪▪▫ Ireland initially banned The Marx Brothers' *Monkey Business* (U.S. 1952) because they thought it would "incite anarchy" in the nation.

- ▪▪▫ Norway banned Monty Python's *Life of Brian* (U.K. 1979) for a year because of blasphemy, but the liberal Swedes gave it the green light, promoting it as "the film that is so funny that it was banned in Norway!"

- ▪▪▫ The antiwar theme of the 1930s' classic *All Quiet on the Western Front* (U.S. 1930) met with a frosty reception from Germany's Nazi party, who released rats into cinemas to scare off moviegoers.

- ▪▪▫ Sweden banned *E.T.* (U.S. 1982) for children under 11, saying the movie showed parents being hostile to their offspring.

- ▪▪▫ Howard Hughes' movie *The Outlaw* (U.S. 1943) was banned for three years in the U.S. because of its constant focus on Jane Russell's breasts.

- ▪▪▫ The original *King Kong* (U.S. 1933) was banned in Finland because the ape resorted to gratuitous and excessive violence.

- ▪▪▪ ***Indiana Jones and the Temple of Doom*** (U.S. 1984) was temporarily banned in India because of a scene where monkey brains are served as a meal. Monkeys are sacred to Hindus.

- ▪▪▪ Thirteen episodes of the U.K. period drama ***Upstairs Downstairs*** (1971–75) were banned in the U.S. because they featured suicide, homosexuality and adultery—subjects thought too daring for family audiences in the 1970s.

- ▪▪▪ The Disney documentary ***The Vanishing Prairie*** (U.S. 1954) was originally banned in New York because it showed a buffalo giving birth.

- ▪▪▪ ***Lara Croft Tomb Raider: The Cradle of Life*** (U.S. 2003) was banned in China for its unflattering portrayal of Chinese society.

- ▪▪▪ The Australian TV series ***Skippy the Bush Kangaroo*** (1966–68) was banned in Sweden for fear that it would mislead children into believing that animals had special powers.

- ▪▪▪ In 1964, China's Peking Cinema Institute banned an educational film titled ***Elementary Safety in Swimming in Rivers*** because they considered the safety element to be a bourgeois tendency likely to undermine the bold revolutionary spirit.

- ▪▪▪ Laurel and Hardy's ***Scram*** (U.S. 1932) was banned in the Netherlands in 1932 by Christian moral watchdogs who claimed that a scene where the pair sat on a bed with a woman to whom neither was married was "indecent."

TV show *Curb Your Enthusiasm* clears man of murder Juan Catalan was cleared of murder in 2003 after outtake footage shot for an episode of *Curb Your Enthusiasm* showed him and his daughter 20 miles (32 km) away watching a baseball game between the Los Angeles Dodgers and the Atlanta Braves at the time of the crime.

The man who wrote down everything he ever did For a minimum of four hours a day, every day, between 1972 and 1996, Robert Shields of Dayton, Washington State, diligently typed out a record of everything that happened to him—no matter how trivial. For example, one entry for July 25, 1993, reads, "7 a.m. I cleaned out the tub and scraped my feet with my fingernails to remove layers of dead skin." He described all the junk mail he received, regularly recorded his temperature and blood pressure and the cost of almost everything he ever bought over a period of 60 years. He even slept in two-hour bursts in order to record his dreams. His 37.5-million-word diary is thought to be the world's longest, dwarfing arguably the most famous diary of all (written by Samuel Pepys 1660–69) by 36.25 million words, and is stored in more than 80 cardboard boxes.

In *Gulliver's Travels*, Jonathan Swift described the two moons of Mars, Phobos and Deimos, giving their exact size and speeds of rotation. He did this more than 100 years before either moon was discovered.

Alan Smithee, the most prolific film director who never existed Between 1968 and 2000, Alan Smithee was credited as the director of nearly 30 movies and numerous episodes of TV series. Yet there was no such person. Instead, he was the official pseudonym used by disenchanted directors who didn't want their name on the credits. Smithee was first credited in the 1969 movie *Death of a Gunfighter*, whose star, Richard Widmark, had sacked the original director, Robert Totten, partway through filming and replaced him with Don Siegel. Neither Totten nor Siegel wanted to

"disenchanted directors"

be credited as director because Widmark had effectively been in charge. Nevertheless, the non-existent Smithee earned praise from noted movie critic Roger Ebert who wrote, "Director Alan Smithee, a name I'm not familiar with, allows his story to unfold naturally." Alan Smithee continued to be kept busy, apparently working with the likes of Burt Reynolds, Angela Lansbury and David Janssen, until in 1998 Eric Idle exploited the in-joke in *An Alan Smithee Film: Burn Hollywood Burn*. Idle played Smithee, who wants to disassociate himself from a movie he has directed, only to find that the one pseudonym he is able to use is his own name. Ironically, the movie's real director, Arthur Hiller, was so dissatisfied with the final cut that he asked for his name to be removed and Alan Smithee was credited as director instead. The movie was a commercial and critical failure, and the negative publicity it attracted drew attention to the long-standing pseudonym. As a result, the Directors Guild of America officially retired Alan Smithee.

The artist Caravaggio was killed by paint Four hundred years after his death in 1610, tests on the bones of Italian artist Caravaggio showed that he probably died of lead poisoning—from his paint. The lead levels in his body were high enough to have driven him insane—he killed a man and was often involved in brawls—and ultimately to have caused his death. He was known to have been particularly messy with his paints.

King Kong was only 18 in (46 cm) high The mighty King Kong from the 1933 classic film was actually only an 18-inch-high (46-cm) model with mechanical joints. When he arrived in New York, he was required to grow to 24 in (61 cm), so that he was bigger than the model buildings. The 1976 version of the tale sold itself on the promise of a real 40-ft (12-m) ape robot terrorizing New York. However, it was an impossible task from the start, and although the robot was constructed, it appeared in only a few seconds of the final movie, replaced by a reliably low-tech human in a gorilla suit.

The world's longest movie is literally *The Cure for Insomnia* at 87 hours What is it about? Directed by John Henry Timmis IV, this movie has no plot but simply consists of artist L.D. Groban reading his poem "A Cure for Insomnia" over the course of 3½ days. Its premiere was in Chicago from January 31–February 3, 1987. Sadly, it was never released to the public, but if it had been put out on DVD it would have filled 22 disks.

The biggest movie flops of the last decade (net losses)

1   **$121.7m**   *Sahara* (U.S. 2005)

2   **$119.1m**   *The Alamo* (U.S. 2004)

3   **$112.8m**   *The Adventures of Pluto Nash* (U.S./Aus 2002)

4   **$106.0m**   *Speed Racer* (U.S./Aus/Ger 2008)

5   **$75.3m**   *The Nutcracker in 3D* (Hun/U.K. 2010)

6   **$71.3m**   *How Do You Know* (U.S. 2010)

7   **$70.4m**   *Treasure Planet* (U.S. 2002)

8   **$68.3m**   *A Sound of Thunder* (U.S./U.K. 2005)

9   **$67.8m**   *Around the World in 80 Days* (U.S. 2004)

10   **$66.7m**   *Gigli* (U.S. 2003)

By comparison, one of the most famous "flops" of recent years, Kevin Costner's *Waterworld* (U.S. 1995), actually made around $90 million profit at the box office.

The authorized biography of Howard Hughes that was a work of fiction The man who launched the career of Jane Russell and once dated some of Hollywood's most famous stars, movie producer Howard Hughes spent the last 15 years of his life as a paranoid recluse. Obsessed with health and hygiene and guarded from outsiders by his hired "Mormon Mafia," he would not allow anyone else to touch his food and even his own doctor was only permitted to examine him from across the room. From 1961 till his death in 1976, he met just three people from the outside world.

> **"last 15 years of his life as a paranoid recluse"**

In December 1970, a *Newsweek* article about the "invisible billionaire" intrigued Clifford Irving, an American author living on the Mediterranean island of Ibiza, who realized that publishers would pay huge sums for an authorized biography of Hughes. Irving knew that there was no way Hughes would cooperate with such a project, so this would be an authorized biography with a difference—one littered with invented material. In short, it would be a fake, but Irving reasoned that Hughes' obsession with privacy meant that it was highly unlikely that he would ever come forward to challenge it. Copying Hughes' handwriting, Irving sent three letters to his publisher, McGraw-Hill, stating that the renowned recluse wanted Irving to write his biography. Unaware of the deception, McGraw-

Hill leaped at the chance and offered Hughes $500,000, along with a generous advance and expenses for Irving. After forging Hughes' signature on the contract, Irving set about making sure that all the money intended for Hughes ended up in his account instead. This entailed photographing his blonde Swiss wife Edith in a black wig, doctoring her spare passport so that it appeared to be the property of H.R. Hughes, and getting her to open a Zurich bank account as "Helga Hughes."

Irving invented nearly a hundred secret meetings with Hughes in 1971 and delivered his finished manuscript in September of that year, only to learn that a former Hughes associate, Robert Easton, was also writing an authorized biography of the great man, which was being serialized in *Life* magazine. Irving responded by creating a telegram from Hughes, denouncing the Easton book as a fake. When word of the rival books reached the Hughes camp, they arranged a press conference—his first in over 15 years—in which reporters in a Los Angeles studio were invited to put questions to him over a direct phone link. Hughes took this opportunity to state that he had never met Irving. In desperation, Irving claimed that the voice on the phone was not Hughes but an imposter.

However, the net was closing in. When a defiant Harold McGraw appeared on TV brandishing three checks cashed by H.R. Hughes, Hughes' lawyer was able to freeze the frame and decipher the name of the Zurich bank. After the bank revealed that H.R. Hughes was a woman, a comparison of photographs exposed "Helga Hughes" as Edith Irving. The game was up. Irving confessed, and he and his wife were jailed. *The Autobiography of Howard Hughes* was never published.

Stalin's grandson has filed numerous legal suits against people who dare to suggest that Stalin was a bad man Yevgeny Dzhugasvili has sued various Russian media outlets for suggesting that his Grampa Joe had been responsible for any deaths while he was Soviet dictator. The exact number of executions that took place under Stalin's regime is disputed, but most figures put it at over 20 million.

Under its Subversive Activities Registration Act, South Carolina law requires groups that intend to overthrow the government to register their details with the authorities and pay $5.

The Icelandic candidate whose campaign was a joke, until he was elected Icelandic comedian Jon Gnarr founded the nation's Best Party as a satirical joke, only to find himself elected mayor of Reykjavik in 2010 on the strength of a campaign that promised a polar bear display for the zoo, free towels at public swimming pools, a Disneyland at the airport and a drug-free Parliament by 2020. Needing a coalition partner, he immediately ruled out any party whose members had not seen all five seasons of *The Wire*. Once in office, Mayor Gnarr started taking his job seriously, although some observers had reservations about a man whose experience of foreign relations amounted to a radio show in which he used to make crank phone calls to the White House, the CIA, the FBI and police stations in the Bronx to see if they had found his lost wallet.

The Pacific islanders who still worship Prince Philip and a U.S. naval officer from World War II The people of the Pacific island of Vanuatu have worshiped a mysterious U.S. naval officer, John Frum, since World War II. On ceremonial occasions they dress as U.S. naval officers and play "The Star Spangled Banner" on bamboo flutes. Villagers on the nearby island of Tanna worship Prince Philip of England—Queen Elizabeth II's husband—who once sent them a signed photograph, which now forms the centerpiece of a mountainside shrine in his honor.

Guantanamo Bay—Cuba never cashed the checks, apart from once, which they say was a mistake The United States pays Cuba over $4,000 a month in rent for the controversial Guantanamo naval base, but Cuba hasn't cashed any of the checks for over 50 years in protest at what it considers the "illegal" occupation by the U.S. Indeed, Fidel Castro recently revealed that only one check has ever been cashed—back in 1959 due to confusion in the early days of the island's revolution.

The Iranian government issued a book of acceptable male hairstyles To help avoid "decadent Western cuts," Iran's culture ministry has released a catalogue of desirable hairstyles for Iranian men. These are uniformly short and neat (with a dash of gel allowed) but definitely no ponytails, Mohawks or mullets. In recent years, men with spiky hair and wearing tight jeans have been arrested by Iranian police, while barber shops have been shut down for offering inappropriate haircuts.

Most bizarre dictators

■■■ **Nicolae Ceauşescu, President of Romania** (1974–89)
Ceauşescu's extreme measures resulted in the deaths of at least 15,000 Romanians a year in the latter half of his rule. Among his crazier edicts were that TV newswomen were banned from wearing jewelry, typewriters could only be owned by license from the government, and books on human reproduction were to be classified as "state secrets." In an attempt to push up the country's birthrate, he introduced a prohibitive "celibacy tax" on childless women, even if they were infertile.

■■■ **François "Papa Doc" Duvalier, President of Haiti** (1957–71)
"Papa Doc" had about 30,000 people killed, often by his roving gangs of thugs called the Tonton Macoutes. He was keen on voodoo, modeling himself on the voodoo god of the dead and basing many of his laws on superstitious beliefs. For example, he ordered all black dogs to be put to death. He also claimed to have killed JFK with a curse. Although he took to wearing dark glasses everywhere, Papa Doc rarely shunned the limelight, ordering that all news stories on national TV be about him.

■■■ **Saparmurat Niyazov, President of Turkmenistan** (1990–2006)
Niyazov was renowned for his egocentric eccentricities. The self-styled "Father of all Turkmen," he renamed a town, a meteor and the month of January after himself, and April—and bread—after his mother. September was renamed "Ruhnama" in honor of a spiritual book he had written, which naturally became compulsory reading in schools and universities and was even part of the nation's driver's exam. He built numerous statues of himself across the country—including a gilded one that rotated to face the sun—and adorned the capital, Ashgabat, with large images of himself. He also declared a national holiday in honor

*of melons. Among the many things he banned were opera,
ballet, the circus, lip-syncing in public, listening to car radios,
video games, smoking, men with long hair or beards, gold teeth,
female news reporters wearing makeup on TV, and all dogs from
Ashgabat because of their "unappealing odor."*

▪▪▪ **Kim Jong-Il, leader of North Korea** (1994–2011)

*Jong-Il was a movie buff with a particular love for James Bond
and Rambo. He owned at least 20,000 DVDs and once kidnapped a
South Korean actress and her director husband, in a bid to start a
North Korean version of Hollywood. He was also fond of alcohol,
spending half a million dollars a year on brandy and boasting
10,000 bottles of wine in his cellar. Fussy about his food, he
hired a member of staff to inspect his rice, because he insisted on
every grain being the same size. His chosen method of transport
was rail, and he owned 19 stations and six luxury trains, three of
which were decoys for security purposes. Although only 5 ft 3 in
(1.6 m) tall, in 1989 he had all short or disabled people deported
from the capital, Pyongyang.*

▪▪▪ **Alexander Lukashenko, President of Belarus** (1994–)

*Like any good dictator, the President of Belarus does not
encourage opposition, and during the 2006 elections he warned
that people attending anti-government protests would have
their necks wrung "as one might a duck." Other opponents were
locked up while two cabinet colleagues who dared to voice an
opinion simply vanished, never to be seen again. Away from the
daily trials of dictatorship, Lukashenko enjoys listening to songs
about himself and is a hockey fanatic who likes to train with
the national team—although anyone attempting to check him
may have to deal with his ever-present armed guards.*

The British government has a wine cellar worth over $3m
To cater for state visits and government hospitality, the British Foreign Office has a cellar hidden beneath a grand London mansion that contains around 39,000 bottles of the finest wines and spirits.

The real Uncle Sam was a meat-packer from Troy, New York, named Samuel Wilson (1766–1854) At the time of the War of 1812, Wilson had obtained a contract to supply beef to the Army. The beef was shipped in barrels, which, as government property, were branded with the initials "U.S." However, soldiers joked that the letters stood for "Uncle Sam" who had supplied the product, and the name stuck. Samuel Wilson's unwitting contribution to America's national symbol was formally recognized by Congress in 1961.

Zimbabwe has 2.5 million phantom voters The electoral roll in Robert Mugabe's Zimbabwe has 2.5 million "extra" names— including no fewer than 41,000 people over the age of 100 in a country where the average life expectancy is 49. Remarkably, 16,800 of these are listed as sharing the same date of birth— January 1, 1901. Other voters on the roll were below two years of age. Richard Johnson of the South African Institute of Race Relations remarked, "This phantom vote is more than enough to settle the outcome of any election, and, if experience is any guide, phantom voters are likely to vote early and often in the next Zimbabwean poll."

Were Mussolini's brain and blood put up for sale on eBay? Well, his granddaughter certainly thought so. In 2009, Alessandra Mussolini complained to police that blood and brains taken from the Italian dictator's body during his 1945 postmortem and subsequently preserved at a Milan hospital were being offered for sale on eBay for $20,000. The advert was quickly withdrawn before any bids could be made because it violated eBay rules forbidding the sale of human organic material, but whether the remains were actually Mussolini's is debatable.

Gerald Ford was the only U.S. president to survive two assassination attempts. He died from natural causes in 2006. Both attackers are still alive and free from prison as of 2010.

Beijing's underground city designed to hold six million people Working mainly by hand, over 300,000 people, including children, were recruited in the 1970s to dig a network of tunnels that cover an area of 33 square miles (85 sq km) beneath Beijing. The underground city of Dixia Cheng was built as a vast bomb shelter at a time when China feared nuclear war with the Soviet Union. The complex, which contains restaurants, clinics, schools, theaters, factories and even a roller-skating rink, is reached via 90 secret entrances hidden in shops in the streets above ground. Part of it was opened as a tourist attraction in 2000.

National security blunders

With these guys in charge, its a miracle we're all still here!

■■■ When Taiwan ordered a consignment of helicopter batteries from the U.S. in 2006, the Pentagon **mistakenly sent nuclear missile fuses** instead.

■■■ An agent with Britain's MI6 accidentally **sold a camera on eBay that contained highly sensitive information**. Instead of the usual holiday snaps, the postal worker who bought the camera was surprised to find pictures of terrorist leaders, missiles, rockets and a document concerning a secret encrypted computer network used by field agents.

■■■ Leaving the 1999 NATO summit in Washington, Bill Clinton left behind arguably the most important piece of luggage in the world—the briefcase known as the nuclear football—which contains **the electronic launch codes to authorize a nuclear attack**. Happily, an aide walked the four blocks back to the White House without being tempted to blow up the world.

■■■ Jimmy Carter preferred to keep the **nuclear launch codes in his jacket pocket** rather than in a briefcase. Unfortunately, he once left them in his suit when it was sent for dry cleaning.

■■■ On the day that her husband Sir John Sawers was appointed the new head of MI6, putting him in charge of British intelligence operations, Lady Shelley Sawers **unwisely used her Facebook page** to post 19 pictures of the couple on vacation. She had put virtually no privacy protection on her account, allowing any old Facebook user to find out the family address, the names of their friends and their favorite haunts. Perhaps most alarmingly, the page also carried pictures of Sir John on the beach in his Speedos.

▪▪▪ Bob Quick, Britain's senior antiterrorist police officer, made the mistake of approaching the Prime Minister's office at 10 Downing Street with **secret plans** detailing imminent antiterrorist raids **clearly visible to waiting press photographers**. His blunder forced the police to carry out the raids earlier than was intended.

The donkey elected to office By virtue of 51 votes cast in 1938, Boston Curtis, the Republican candidate, was elected precinct committeeman for Milton, Washington State—to the great amusement of Milton's Democrat mayor Kenneth Simmons. For he had sponsored Curtis—a large brown mule with long ears—partly to mock the Republicans, but also to prove his point that people have no idea whom they're voting for.

U.S. Senator Strom Thurmond once gave a filibuster speech that lasted for 24 hours and 18 minutes Thurmond, at one point the longest serving senator in history, failed in his objective to hold up the 1957 Civil Rights bill that aimed to help black citizens vote. Senators present were forced to sleep in the chamber on cots brought from a local hotel as Thurmond talked tirelessly on such fascinating matters as the election laws of all 48 states and his grandmother's recipes. He only sat down after his doctor advised him against kidney damage should he continue.

Even the color of politicians' ties matters to them—blue is viewed as trustworthy, red is aggressive.

Ballet dancer Margot Fonteyn was a failed revolutionary Information released recently by Britain's National Archives reveals that the plot to overthrow the pro-U.S. government of Panama in 1959 had an unlikely figure at its heart—world-famous ballet dancer Dame Margot Fonteyn. She didn't exactly swap her tutu for battle fatigues, but instead she and her Panamanian husband, Roberto Arias,

"land arms and men on the shores of Panama"

used a fishing vacation as cover to land arms and men on the shores of Panama. However, the Panamanian military quickly got wind of the coup and as the plot descended into chaos, Fonteyn panicked. She threw overboard what she believed to be incriminating letters, but which were actually just white armbands intended to distinguish the rebels when they landed. When her blunder came to light, the letters were hastily buried, along with machine guns and ammunition, but the Panamanians found them and Fonteyn was arrested. She was put in prison where, in accordance with her status, she was given a spacious cell with fresh flowers. Despite the overwhelming evidence against her, she was freed a day later and allowed to leave the country. The British ambassador to Panama condemned the ballerina's "irresponsible" behavior. Following a change in government, Arias was allowed to return to Panama, but was partially paralyzed in an assassination attempt in 1964. Fonteyn, too, returned to Panama to care for her husband until his death in 1989. She died there two years later.

Boris Yeltsin in his underpants outside the White House

According to reports, President Clinton told a journalist that Russian Premier Boris Yeltsin was once found standing outside the White House in his underwear in an inebriated state, having eluded his secret service guards. He was trying to find a taxi to take him to a restaurant. On another occasion, Mr. Yeltsin was mistaken for an intruder by the secret service after drunkenly stumbling into the basement of his Washington residence.

The United States and the Soviet Union were only two miles from each other

The island of Little Diomede, part of the U.S., sits in the Bering Strait between Siberia and Alaska. Just two miles west of Little Diomede is the island of Big Diomede, part of the former Soviet Union—too close for comfort for both parties.

U.S. presidents' wealth

Taking into account land assets, savings, inheritance, homes, earned salaries, book royalties and ownership of companies, how much in today's dollars were U.S. presidents worth?

1	John F. Kennedy	*$1 billion*
2	George Washington	*$525 million*
3	Thomas Jefferson	*$212 million*
4	Theodore Roosevelt	*$125 million*
5	Andrew Jackson	*$119 million*
6	James Madison	*$101 million*
7	Lyndon B. Johnson	*$98 million*
8	Herbert Hoover	*$75 million*
9	Franklin D. Roosevelt	*$60 million*
10	John Tyler	*$51 million*
11	Bill Clinton	*$38 million*
12	James Monroe	*$27 million*
13	Martin Van Buren	*$26 million*
14	Grover Cleveland	*$25 million*
15	George Bush	*$23 million*
16	John Quincy Adams	*$21 million*
17	George W. Bush	*$20 million*
18	John Adams	*$19 million*
19	Richard Nixon	*$15 million*

20	Ronald Reagan	*$13 million*
21	James Knox Polk	*$10 million*
22	Dwight D. Eisenhower	*$8 million*
23	Gerald Ford	*$7 million*
	Jimmy Carter	
25	Zachary Taylor	*$6 million*
26	William Henry Harrison	*$5 million*
	Benjamin Harrison	
	Barack Obama	
29	Millard Fillmore	*$4 million*
30	Rutherford Birchard Hayes	*$3 million*
	William Howard Taft	
32	Franklin Pierce	*$2 million*
33	William McKinley	*$1 million*
	Warren Harding	
35	James Buchanan	*under $1 million*
	Abraham Lincoln	
	Andrew Johnson	
	Ulysses Simpson Grant	
	James Garfield	
	Chester Arthur	
	Woodrow Wilson	
	Calvin Coolidge	
	Harry S. Truman	

The Soviet who might have averted nuclear war in 1962
You've probably never heard of Vasili Alexandrovich Arkhipov, but he might just have been the man who saved the world. In October 1962, at the height of the Cuban Missile Crisis, the former farm boy was deputy commander of a Soviet submarine carrying antiship nuclear torpedoes. The U.S. had set up a naval blockade of Communist Cuba, but Arkhipov's sub (along with three others) had orders to sneak through and establish a secret base on the island. To try to force the Soviet subs to the surface for identification, U.S. destroyers dropped practice depth charges, a bombardment that panicked the captain of Arkhipov's sub, Valentin Savitsky, to conclude that the war must already have started. So, Savitsky ordered the assembly of one of the nuclear torpedoes, to make it ready to take aim at the destroyers.

"U.S. destroyers dropped practice depth charges"

But Moscow's rules of engagement stipulated that a captain needed the backing of his two most senior officers before he could actually fire a nuclear weapon. The sub's political officer said yes; Arkhipov said no. Instead of nuking the Americans, the sub was forced to surface and flee back to the U.S.S.R. Nuclear war had been averted—on the word of one man.

Arab alpha male—Sheikh Hamad bin Hamdan Al Nahyan owns the world's largest jeep, and that's not all His specially built, 21-ft-tall (6.4-m) Willys jeep is four times normal size and weighs 4.4 tons even without the engine. Due to its size, it can't be driven from the cabin—instead the driver has to sit behind the seven-slat grille. It's impossible to say why anyone would want a jeep that big, but the sheikh certainly isn't somebody who does things by halves...

- ▪▪▪ He once built the **world's largest truck**—a replica Dodge Power Wagon eight times the size of the original model and weighing over 50 tons. It has four bedrooms inside the cabin.

- ▪▪▪ He constructed a **motor home** in the shape of a giant globe that is exactly **one-millionth the size of planet Earth**.

- ▪▪▪ He owns over 200 cars and trucks, and stores them in his **own personal pyramid** outside Abu Dhabi.

- ▪▪▪ In 1983, he bought **seven Mercedes 500 SEL cars, one for each day of the week**, and had them painted in the colors of the rainbow with matching interiors. Gun racks held M16 rifles, which were painted to match the cars.

- ▪▪▪ He has carved his name in letters 1,640 ft high (500 m) on **his own island**, Futaisi Island, in the U.A.E. The word "HAMAD" measures 2 miles (3 km) across and was crafted in the sand by a crew of workers over several weeks. The letters are dug so deep that they form waterways, and the inscription can even be seen from space.

The New Zealand spy who lied on his résumé The man hired as chief of New Zealand's Defence Technology Agency, giving him access to highly classified intelligence, resigned five years later after being exposed as a fantasist who had told outrageous lies on his résumé. British-born Stephen Wilce claimed to have been a Royal Marine, a former Olympic bobsleigh team member, the designer of the Polaris missile guidance system, a helicopter pilot with Prince Andrew, a member of the Welsh Rugby Union team, and a spy with British intelligence—but these claims all turned out to be false. Wilce, described by one previous employer as a "Walter Mitty character," told investigators that he had been making up tall stories about himself since he was a child.

China thinks that Sweden has a town where only women are allowed China's state-run Xinhua news agency has reported the existence of a remote town in northern Sweden where no men are permitted. Xinhua says that men attempting to enter Chako Paul City, apparently founded in 1820 by a wealthy, man-hating widow, are "beaten half to death" by police, while many of the 25,000 women in the city become lesbians "because they could not suppress their sexual needs." Mystified Swedish tourism officials say they have never even heard of

> **"founded by a wealthy man-hating widow"**

Chako Paul City. "At 25,000 residents, the town would be one of the largest in northern Sweden," said a spokesman. "I find it hard to believe that you could keep something like that a secret for more than 150 years."

Jimmy Carter mistranslated President Carter's December 1977 visit to Poland remains memorable only for the efforts of his official translator, Steven Seymour. Stepping from his plane at Warsaw Airport, the President spoke innocently of his "desires for the future," but Seymour's tortured Polish meant that the crowds were informed instead that Carter had "lusts for the future." Worse was to follow when Carter's casual remark that he wished the Polish people well was translated by Seymour into an assertion that the President "desires the Poles carnally." The confused Poles were finally told that the President had "left America never to return." Fast becoming an object of ridicule in Polish eyes, Carter replaced Seymour with Jerzy Krycki, but Krycki's problem was that he couldn't understand the President's English! All in all, it was a state trip to forget.

U.S. officials thought Switzerland had a navy Arranging an international ceremony to mark the completion of the Panama Canal in 1914, the U.S. State Department sent an invitation to the Swiss Navy. When it was pointed out that Switzerland was a landlocked nation and therefore had no navy, red-faced officials swiftly withdrew the invitation.

Craziest true CIA plots

Acoustic Kitty

At the height of the Cold War in the 1960s, the CIA surgically altered a cat so that it could serve as a secret agent. For operation *Acoustic Kitty*, the cat was slit open and wired up to become a walking bugging device in the hope that it could listen to secret conversations from window sills, park benches or garbage cans. Batteries and a microphone were inserted into the cat's body and an antenna was placed in its tail, but at first the cat had a tendency to abandon its covert security mission in order to chase mice. So, another wire was inserted to override hunger pangs. Finally, the cat was ready for its first live trial. In 1966, CIA operatives took the animal to a Washington park, let it out of the van and listened eagerly on their headphones—as the cat crossed the road and was run over by a taxi. *Acoustic Kitty* was dead. Five years' design and an estimated $20 million of technology had been destroyed in a matter of seconds.

French bread

In 1951, the CIA is said to have spiked bread in a picturesque French village with the hallucinogenic drug LSD as part of a covert mind control experiment during the Cold War. The Americans were looking into the possibility of using the drug to manipulate prisoners and enemy forces mentally. Hundreds of villagers in Pont-Saint-Esprit were affected—at least five died and dozens were locked up after going insane.

▪▪▪ Berlin tunnel

1953's *Operation Gold* was an attempt to hack into the phone lines of the Soviet headquarters in East Berlin. Six months was spent digging a 1,476-ft-long (450-m) tunnel, allowing the CIA to listen in to 50,000 conversations in the next 12 months. Little did they know that the KGB had been tipped off in advance and were feeding them bogus information the whole time.

▪▪▪ Pigeon missile

Project Pigeon represented American behaviorist B.F. Skinner's efforts to develop a pigeon-guided missile during World War II. A pigeon was packed into a missile, and a lens on the front of the missile projected an image of the target onto a screen inside. There, the pigeon, which had been trained to recognize the target, was supposed to peck at the screen. If the pecks were in the center of the screen, the missile would continue to fly straight; if the pecks were to the side, it would change course. The most remarkable aspect to the story is that $25,000 was spent on *Project Pigeon* before anyone realized it was a crazy idea.

The New York housewife who received the President's calls
In 1965, a succession of highly confidential international calls meant for the White House ended up being answered instead by Mrs. Rose Brown, a New York housewife. The confusion arose because the number for her home in Queens was the same as that of the White House, and her area code for long-distance dialing was almost identical—202 for Washington and 212 for New York. On hearing that his calls had been going astray, President Lyndon B. Johnson wrote to Mrs. Brown saying: "I couldn't be more gratified to know that you are handling these calls with all the diplomacy of an ambassador." In return, the President promised to be equally tactful if receiving any calls meant for the Brown family.

The man who invaded the Soviet Union on his own In an attempt to create an "imaginary bridge" between the East and the West during the Cold War, an 18-year-old West German amateur pilot flew across Europe and daringly landed his light aircraft near Moscow's Red Square. On the morning of May 28, 1987, Mathias Rust, with barely 50 hours' flying experience to his name, took off from an airport in Helsinki, Finland, telling air traffic control that he was going to Stockholm, Sweden. Instead, he headed east and turned off all his communications equipment. Over the following hours he kept disappearing from the radar, leading to wholesale confusion on the ground. Finally at around 7 p.m. he reached the skies above Moscow. His original intention was to land inside the Kremlin, but he reasoned that the KGB would simply arrest him and deny the incident. There were too many people to land safely in Red Square, so he chose to touch down on a nearby bridge. A series of wires would normally have prevented him from landing there, but as luck would have it, they had been removed for maintenance for that day only. Passers-by appeared bemused at seeing an aircraft in the heart of the capital, but it wasn't long before Rust was arrested. He was sentenced to four years in prison but was released early as a goodwill gesture. Unlikely though it

> **"bring about the end of the Cold War"**

may seem, Rust's solo invasion did help bring about the end of the Cold War. His flight irreparably damaged the reputation of the feared Soviet military and allowed the country's reforming President, Mikhail Gorbachev, to remove many of his fiercest opponents from positions of power.

India's living dead want their rights back On June 30, 2010, more than 500 supposedly dead people from Upper Pradesh, India, staged a rally to show that they were still very much alive. The "Day of Rebirth" was organized by Lal Bihari, who first discovered he was officially dead in 1976 when he tried to apply for a bank loan. His uncle had bribed an Indian government official to register Bihari as dead in order to seize ownership of his land. In 2003, Bihari was awarded the Ig Nobel Peace Prize for three outstanding achievements relating to his situation. First, for leading an active life even though he has been declared dead by the government. Second, for waging a lively posthumous campaign against bureaucratic inertia and greedy relatives. And third, for creating the Association of Dead People.

Russia used to own Alaska In 1733, Alaska was colonized by Russia, but the Russian government eventually lost interest in the distant outpost and in 1867 sold it to the U.S. for $7.2 million (2¢ per acre). Thirteen years later, gold was discovered in Alaska.

Politicians with foot-in-mouth disease

- ▪▪▪ "More and more of our imports come from overseas." **George W. Bush**

- ▪▪▪ "For 7½ years I've worked alongside President Reagan. We've had triumphs. Made some mistakes. We've had some sex—uh—setbacks." **George Bush**

- ▪▪▪ "Outside of the killings, [Washington] D.C., has one of the lowest crime rates in the country." **Mayor Marion Barry**

- ▪▪▪ "I believe we are on an irreversible trend toward more freedom and democracy. But that could change." **Dan Quayle**

▪▪▫ "This is the worst disaster in California since I was elected." **Governor Pat Brown**

▪▪▫ "I have opinions of my own—strong opinions—but I don't always agree with them." **George Bush**

▪▪▫ "You read what Disraeli had to say. I don't remember what he said. He said something. He's no longer with us." **Bob Dole**

▪▪▫ "We understand the importance of having the bondage between the parent and the child." **Dan Quayle**

▪▪▫ "It's no exaggeration to say the undecideds could go one way or the other." **George Bush**

▪▪▫ "I didn't go down there with any plan for the Americas, or anything. I went down there to find out from them and their views. You'd be surprised; they're all individual countries." **Ronald Reagan**

▪▪▫ "My vision is to make the most diverse state on Earth, and we have people from every planet on the Earth in this state." **Gray Davis, Governor of California**

▪▪▫ "Our enemies are innovative and resourceful, and so are we. They never stop thinking about new ways to harm our country and our people, and neither do we." **George W. Bush**

Sperm whale vomit—a priceless delicacy for centuries
Who would think that vomit could be worth up to $20 a gram?
It is if it comes from the innards of a sperm whale. It's called
ambergris and is so valuable that a 32-lb (14.5-kg) lump of the
stuff found on a beach by an Australian couple in 2006 was
expected to net them close to $300,000—and all because a
whale had a touch of indigestion. So, what is it about sperm
whale vomit that sets it apart from the tomato and diced

**"known
as floating
gold"**

carrot that populates its human
counterpart? Firstly, it is
extremely rare and can float on
the ocean for years before
washing ashore. Also, it is said
to boast medicinal proper-
ties and in the Middle Ages
was used to treat everything from colds to epilepsy. Being
a natural pheromone, it is still eaten by Middle Eastern men
as an aphrodisiac; the libidinous King Charles II of England
consumed it in his breakfast eggs. It is also highly prized as a
spice. Indeed, the chief reason Portugal seized the Maldives in
the 16th century was to gain access to the islands' rich bounty
of the waste matter known as "floating gold." However, its
main use today is in perfumes.

But before you rush to the nearest beach in search
of some ambergris for your partner, be aware that it
has to be exposed to sun and salt water for at least
ten years before it acquires a smooth texture with a sweet,
musky scent. Before that it is soft, black and smells foul—a
bit like excrement.

Cannibal dinner apology In a heartfelt statement, the inhabitants of Erromango Island, Vanuatu, apologized in 2009 to descendants of 19th-century English missionary Reverend John Williams, on behalf of islanders who killed and ate him in 1839.

Russia finally decides that beer is alcoholic Russian President Dmitry Medvedev has signed a bill that, for the first time, officially classifies beer as alcoholic. Previously, anything in Russia containing less than 10% alcohol was considered a foodstuff, so no surprise that there are at least seven million alcoholics in Russia and that the nation's alcohol consumption is already twice the critical level set by the World Health Organization. Almost half of all deaths of working age men in Russia are the result of excessive alcohol consumption—and it's not just vodka. The sale of men's aftershave had to be banned before lunchtime in Moscow because so many alcoholics were drinking the stuff.

You can get addicted to carrots A 1996 edition of the *Australia and New Zealand Journal of Psychiatry* reported the case of a 49-year-old woman who was a carrot junkie. She experienced sensations of carrot craving and withdrawal usually associated with smoking, apparently becoming irritable and nervous if she couldn't get her daily fix of carrots. Scientists say it's all down to beta carotene, the chemical pigment that makes carrots orange.

Man eats deadly snake for a bet After killing a venomous snake with stones, Indian farm laborer Zaver Rathod proceeded to eat the entire snake raw for a bet. No surprise, he soon felt very ill, but luckily doctors managed to remove the snake from his stomach before the venom could enter his bloodstream.

Early Europeans were cannibals Scientists who have been studying 800,000-year-old fossil bones found in a Spanish cave have concluded that early Europeans ate human meat as part of their everyday diet. It appears that the brains of children were considered a particular delicacy.

The Great Molasses Disaster It sounds like an urban legend, but it really happened: on January 15, 1919, a large molasses storage tank burst in the North End district of Boston, Massachusetts, sending a 15-ft-high (4.5-m) tsunami-like wave of molasses surging through neighboring streets at a speed of 35 mph (56 km/h), killing 21 people and injuring 150. The accident occurred in a 2,300,000-gallon tank at the Purity Distillery Company, and witnesses said the explosion sounded like a rumbling train coupled with machine gun fire as rivets shot out of the tank. The molasses wave was so powerful it destroyed buildings in its path, broke the girders of a nearby bridge and lifted a train off the tracks. Soon the streets were covered in a waist-deep sticky mass, which trapped and killed several horses. People were hurled through the air and a truck was dumped into Boston Harbor. It took over 87,000 man hours to clean up the mess, but even nearly a century later residents claim that on hot summer days the area still smells of molasses.

In Mauritania, fat is the new thin Young girls are forced to drink gallons of milk, butter and millet to fatten themselves up for marriage because in that part of Africa wealth and beauty are measured in terms of a woman's weight.

New Zealanders serve up horse semen If you want a milk shake in New Zealand, make sure that you're not really drinking horse semen. Christchurch racehorse breeder Lindsay Kerslake has been marketing the semen shots in flavors including vanilla, strawberry and chocolate. They're supposed to taste like a milk shake and be washed down with an energy drink chaser, a combination designed to give you the stamina of a stallion for the next seven days.

Paris 1870, when elephant, camel and bear were on the Christmas menu For over four months from September 1870 to January 1871, Paris was under siege from Prussian troops at the height of the Franco–Prussian War. The severe shortage of food meant that Parisians were slaughtered whatever animals caught their eye, including Castor and Pollux, two elephants from the city zoo. A menu for Christmas 1870 offered such delights as stuffed donkey's head, elephant consommé, roast camel, kangaroo stew, antelope terrine, bear ribs, and wolf haunch in deer sauce. Of course, being the French they even managed to make these dishes sound appetizing. Who would not be tempted by "Civet de chat aux champignons" (cat)? Or "Brochettes de foie de chien à la maître d'hôtel" (dog)? Or "Gigots de chien flanqués de ratons. Sauce poivrade" (dog again, this time with a side dish of rat)?

Scientists say men are more turned on by a curry than by their partner British scientists have discovered that men become more emotionally aroused while eating a curry than when kissing their partner. By stimulating heat sensors in the mouth and throat, capsaicin, the substance that provides the heat in hot curries, increases the brain's output of endorphins, leading to a sense of overwhelming euphoria.

Sixty percent of the world's adults cannot digest milk.

Death row inmate to become fish food If Gene Hathorn, a convicted killer who has been on death row in Texas since 1985, loses his final appeal against execution, he has agreed to let Danish-based Chilean artist Marco Evaristti turn his body into fish food. Evaristti plans to deep-freeze Hathorn's body and then stage an exhibition where visitors can feed hundreds of goldfish with food made from the human corpse. Evaristti is no stranger to unconventional food. In 2007, he held a dinner party where the main course consisted of meatballs made partly with fat removed from his own body by liposuction.

Eating live octopus—a Korean delicacy—can kill you by asphyxiation You have to be careful when eating live octopus because the tentacles stick to any surface they touch. They will cling to your chopsticks, your teeth, the roof of your mouth and your tongue as the octopus tries to hang on to life, and if you don't chew them thoroughly, the suction cups will stick to your throat and cause you to choke.

Drinkers live longer than teetotalers At last some research we can take comfort from. A recent study conducted by the University of Texas shows that nondrinkers often die early because they tend to be lonely, depressed, poor and stressed out.

Who's for a glass of seagull wine? As an appealing drink, seagull wine sounds on par with battery acid, but the Inuit people swear by it. It is made by inserting a freshly deceased seagull into a bottle, filling the bottle with water and allowing the liquid to ferment in the sun. Although it is said to be extremely alcoholic, it seems that the main reason the Inuit chose seagulls as the base for their brew is that there are a lot of them about.

Tasty but deadly

▪▪▪ **Amanita mushrooms** The "Destroying Angel," as it is known, looks like a regular mushroom, but it is highly toxic and can cause bloody diarrhea, violent vomiting, extreme stomach pain and eventually death. There are no known antidotes, and even those who have survived eating it have had to undergo a liver transplant.

▪▪▪ **Castor beans** Just chewing two beans of the castor oil plant can be enough to kill you because they contain ricin, the most toxic of all natural poisons, which is 200 times more deadly than cyanide. The poison is concentrated under the bean's shell, and is only effective if the shell is broken or chewed open. Beans swallowed whole can pass through the body without causing any harm.

▪▪▪ **Cassava** Widely grown as a crop in tropical countries, the edible starchy root of cassava is one of the world's major sources of carbohydrates. However, the roots and leaves should never be eaten raw because they contain cyanide —and just 40 mg of pure cassava cyanogenic glucoside is enough to kill a cow.

▪▪▪ **Barbados nut** The seeds of the Barbados nut plant taste so good that you want to eat more. You do so at your own risk, however, for each seed is made up of at least 55% "Hell oil," a poisonous substance that can result in death, particularly among children.

▪▫▪ **Puffer fish** The poison of the puffer fish, tetraodontoxin, is found in the fish's ovaries and is not destroyed by cooking. However, if you remember to remove the entrails and wash the cavity thoroughly before cooking, the fish is perfectly harmless. If you don't, there's a 50% mortality rate—usually within a couple of hours. On average about 50 people a year die from puffer fish poisoning in Japan, and *fugu*, as the Japanese call puffer fish, is the only food the Emperor of Japan is forbidden from eating—for his own safety.

▪▫▪ **Ackee fruit** The national fruit of Jamaica, the ackee is a staple of many dishes, but while the fruit is rich in essential fatty acids, Vitamin A and protein, its unripened seeds and pods are toxic, and are responsible for the condition called Jamaican vomiting sickness. Extreme cases may produce seizures, coma or death.

The pilgrims landed at Plymouth because they ran out of beer 17th-century sailors relied heavily on beer, the standard ration onboard ship being at least two pints a day. It wasn't especially alcoholic but, having been boiled, was probably safer to drink than ordinary water. Also it wasn't perishable, and so no self-respecting captain took to the high seas without a cargo of dozens of barrels of beer. *The Mayflower* was no exception, but her voyage across the Atlantic had been delayed by bad weather and then the captain got lost, as a result of which the ship's supply of beer was running ominously low. So the pilgrims landed at the first place they could find—Plymouth. This is confirmed by an entry in the diary of one of the pilgrims: "We could not now take time for further search... our victuals being much spent, especially our beer." The settlers might not have found a pub that was open, but they quickly learned from their Indian neighbors how to make beer from maize. Breweries soon sprouted up throughout the colonies, and experienced brewers were recruited from London to keep the beer flowing.

Living on beer for Lent It sounds like every beer lover's dream: Iowa newspaper editor J. Wilson went on a beer-and-water-only diet for the 46 days of Lent 2011. To give his scheme historical credibility and to counter any accusations that he just wanted an excuse to drink a lot of beer, he revealed that he got the idea from a tradition practiced by German monks 300 years ago. He then developed a recipe for a high-calorie beer that served as breakfast, lunch and dinner. He drank four 12-oz (340-ml) beers a day during the working week and five bottles on weekends, and insists that he never once got drunk. Not only that, but he lost 30 lb (14 kg) in weight.

There's a new Indian soft drink—cow urine Hindus view cows as sacred and use the animal's urine to cure a range of illnesses from liver disease to obesity and even cancer. So, when they were looking for a new health drink, what could be more natural than cow pee? Although, as with all the best soft drinks, the actual formula is a closely guarded secret, we are promised that it will contain a few herbs and, more importantly, that it definitely won't smell or taste like urine.

It's not illegal to sell food containing insect legs, rat poop and mouse urine, just don't put too much in According to guidelines issued by the U.S. Food and Drug Administration, items presenting no health hazards for humans include oregano plants containing 1 mg of "mammalian excreta" per pound, ground oregano containing an average of five rodent hairs per 10 grams, and peanut butter with 30 insect fragments per 100 grams.

Carrots used to be purple Orange carrots first became popular in 17th-century Netherlands, where they were grown in honor of William of Orange.

Death by sherry enema Texan Michael Warner died of alcohol poisoning after receiving a sherry enema. He had been addicted to enemas since he was a child and also had a serious drinking problem. A medical condition made it painful for him to swallow liquor, so he used to get his fix by administering wine or sherry enemas. However, in 2004 the dose proved fatal, producing a blood alcohol level almost six times the state's legal driving limit.

Pica is a compulsion to eat the inedible. Here are some of the most extreme cases around.

▪▪▪ *A man suffered* **lead** *poisoning because of his fondness for eating roofing plates. Another man was struck down with the same illness after swallowing over 200 live bullets.*

▪▪▪ The New England Journal of Medicine *reported a case where doctors found 12 lb (5.4 kg) of* **coins, needles and necklaces** *in a patient's stomach.*

▪▪▪ *A man in China has eaten more than 440 lb (200 kg) of* **glass** *since he was 20. He eats glass twice a week and is very partial to teacup glass as well as lightbulbs.*

▪▪▪ *Surgeons in Chicago removed a 10-lb (4.5-kg) hairball from the stomach of an 18-year-old woman who suffered from trichophagia, the compulsive eating of* **hair.**

▪▪▪ *A woman in the U.K. swallowed £175.32 of* **loose change** *and in addition to coins she also ate* **metal nuts, wire, pieces of plastic, dog conditioning powder and dried flowers**.

▪▪▪ *When a man in Peru complained of stomach pains, doctors removed 17 metal objects from his stomach—including* **screws, nails, bolts, pens, a knife, a watch clasp and barbed wire.**

▪▪▪ *The Glore Psychiatric Museum in St. Joseph, Missouri, exhibits*

1,446 peculiar items retrieved from the intestines and stomach of a woman—including **453 nails, 42 screws and a number of spoons, safety pins and salt-and-pepper-shaker tops.**

▪▫▫ *A Chinese woman claims to have stayed healthy by eating* **soil and mud** *for over 40 years.*

Coca-Cola didn't really invent Santa Claus A theory exists that the popular image of Santa Claus as we know him today was nothing more than a marketing tool devised by Coca-Cola in the 1930s to boost sales to children, in particular during the winter. You know the one: jolly old Santa with his flowing white beard, wearing the company colors of red and white, and clutching a bottle of Coke. In fact, that depiction of Santa (without the bottle of Coke) had been around since at least the start of the 20th century.

The people who don't need to eat A cult called the Breatharians claim that they do not need food or drink, but can survive solely on the air that they breathe. Their spiritual leader Jasmuheen (a Brisbane mother previously known as Ellen Greve) insists she has eaten little more than herbal tea, juice and an occasional biscuit since 1993, existing on fewer than 300 calories a day. She says she draws her energy from prana—a Hindu term for the universal life force—and meditation, and even claims that her DNA has changed to take in more hydrogen. She and her followers believe that the energy they save on metabolizing food and fluid can be redirected into physical, emotional and spiritual energy. However, three deaths have been linked to her cult, leading critics to condemn the fasting regime as "dangerous." Since failing a 1999 TV test (called off after four days when she displayed symptoms of acute dehydration, stress and high blood pressure), Jasmuheen has resisted all calls to verify her claims. Amid suspicions that she may sneak out for the odd burger, in 2000 she was awarded the Bent Spoon Award by Australian Skeptics "presented to the perpetrator of the most preposterous piece of paranormal or pseudoscientific piffle."

The biggest Chinese restaurant in the world—the West Lake in Changsha—has 5,000 seats and 300 chefs. Each week, it serves 3 tons of fish, 3,600 ducks, 700 chickens, 200 snakes and a ton of pork.

Modern cannibals of New Guinea In a region where Nelson Rockefeller's son disappeared in 1961 and his body was never found, the Korowai people of Papua New Guinea are believed to be among the last tribes in the world to practice cannibalism. In 2006, *60 Minutes* claimed that when someone in Korowai society is accused of being a *khakhua* or sorcerer, he or she is tried, and, if found guilty, decapitated, dismembered, cooked like a pig and eaten, the individual body parts wrapped in banana leaves. Everything is eaten, except for teeth, hair, fingernails, toenails and penis, the favored piece being the brain, which is devoured while still fresh and warm, although pregnant women and children don't join in the feast. Traditionally, the head is eaten by the family of the sorcerer's killer, as a perk. Locals have apparently compared the taste of human flesh to young cassowary, which at least proves that not everything weird tastes like chicken. The Korowai defend the custom by saying that they no longer eat humans, only *khakhua*. However, it has also been claimed that some tribespeople have been encouraged to say that cannibalism is still practiced in order to promote Western tourism.

> **"devoured while still fresh and warm"**

Cheese with maggots is a traditional dish in Sardinia

Casu Marzu cheese, a delicacy on the Italian island of Sardinia, is not considered ready to eat until it is fully infested with the maggot larvae of the cheese fly. The maggots give the cheese a nice moist texture and it packs a kick, too, as the larvae can jump 6 in (15 cm) when disturbed. All the time they are still wriggling, the cheese (including the maggots) is okay to eat, provided you have a strong stomach. If the maggots aren't wriggling, it means the cheese has become toxic and should be thrown out. It all brings a whole new meaning to "pub grub."

Solution to the quiz on page 33

House	1	2	3	4	5
Color	Yellow	Blue	Red	Ivory	Green
Nationality	Norwegian	Ukrainian	English	Spanish	Japanese
Drink	Water	Tea	Milk	Orange juice	Coffee
Smoke	Kools	Chesterfield	Old Gold	Lucky Strike	Parliament
Pet	Fox	Horse	Snails	Dog	Zebra

If you got it right, pat yourself on the back. It has been claimed that only 2% of the population can solve it.

Acknowledgments

9 © Andrisr/Shutterstock.com; 16 © Aleksandr Volodin/iStock.com; 40 © Petro Teslenko/iStock.com; 50 © Good Vector/Shutterstock.com; 54 © Vera Kalinovska/iStock.com; 68 © Perysty/Fotolia.com; 78 © Jennifer Adkins/iStock.com; 90 © Anna Liza Dala/iStock.com; 103 © Dmitry Skvorcov\Fotolia.com; 109 © Simon/Fotolia.com; 120 © Skipan/Fotolia.com; 130 © Yang MingQi/Fotolia.com; 137 © WilleeCole/Shutterstock.com; 140 © Anna Liza Dala/iStock.com; 148 © Theresa Tibbetts/iStock.com; 179 © Harijs A./Shutterstock.com; 193 © Miguel Angel Salinas Salinas/Shutterstock.com; 206 © Anna Tyukhmeneva/Shutterstock.com; 235 © Rozhkovs/Shutterstock.com

If you enjoyed the unbelievable facts and features in this book, take a trip to one of 31 Ripley's Odditoriums worldwide, from New York to South Korea, and see some of the weirdest things on Earth, up close. For more details visit **www.ripleys.com**

For something closer to home, check out our *Ripley's Believe It or Not* annuals, full of stunning images and even more incredible stories, lists and remarkable individuals. The annual and Ripley's other titles are available in hardback format and ebook for digital devices.

Also look out for Ripley's bizarre and entertaining interactive mobile apps. Why not try out the sword swallowing app—Ripley iSword!

Available on iPhone/iPod Touch/iPad
www.ripleys.com/qrisword